Populist Cartoons

Worth Robert Miller

Populist Cartoons

An Illustrated History of the
Third-Party Movement in the 1890s

Truman State University Press

Cover: "The Situation: The Result of Interest Bearing Bonds and Sherman." *Sound Money* (Massillon, OH), August 22, 1895.

Cover design: Teresa Wheeler
Type: Minion Pro © Adobe Systems Inc.; OptimumDTC
Printed by: Sheridan Books, Ann Arbor, Michigan USA

Library of Congress Cataloging-in-Publication Data

Miller, Worth Robert, 1943–
Populist cartoons : an illustrated history of the third-party movement in the 1890s / Worth Robert Miller.
    p. cm.
Includes index.
ISBN 978-1-935503-05-7 (pbk. : alk. paper) — ISBN 978-1-61248-010-7 (electronic)
1. Populist Party (U.S.)—History. 2. Populist Party (U.S.)—History—Caricatures and cartoons. 3. Populism—United States—History—19th century. 4. Populism—United States—History—19th century—Caricatures and cartoons. 5. United States—Politics and government—1865–1933. 6. United States—Politics and government—1865–1933—Caricatures and cartoons. I. Title.
JK2372.M55 2011
324.2732'7—dc22

                                                                        2010051226

Contents

Preface

I FIRST CAME INTO EXTENSIVE CONTACT with Populist cartoons while research-
ing my dissertation on the People's Party in the Oklahoma Territory. Very few
Populists left relevant materials to elite institutions like university archives; therefore, newspapers on microfilm and quantification proved to be the best primary
resources for that, and almost any other, project on Populism. When it came time
to select illustrations for my *Oklahoma Populism* manuscript for publication, I
decided illustrations from Populist newspapers would be far more interesting
and entertaining than the usual photographs of stodgy, bearded old politicians.
The reviewers agreed. Unfortunately, only a few of the cartoons I had collected
were presentable enough to be used in that book; computer technology has now
advanced to the point where the scratch marks, grit, and distortions that inevitably mar microfilmed newspapers can be eliminated.

State press associations founded the Oklahoma Historical Society in 1893
and the Kansas Historical Society in 1875. Almost every newspaper published in
those states afterward placed its historical society on their exchange lists, resulting in two of the most complete state newspaper collections in existence. Most
of the cartoons in this book are from Kansas, Colorado, and Texas. The Kansas
Historical Society also has the most complete edition of the *Southern Mercury*
(Dallas), the most important Populist newspaper in Texas.

In 1997, Missouri State University's chapter of Phi Alpha Theta national
honor society asked me to speak at their annual initiation dinner. I decided the
occasion warranted something both scholarly and entertaining, so I put together
a presentation explaining American Populism through cartoons drawn from
third-party newspapers. The response was so positive that I decided to pursue
the project further. The encouragement of my friend and colleague William G.
Piston was crucial at this point. My student Mathew F. Vaughn introduced me to
a graphics program that could be used to clean up the illustrations. During the
2000/2001 academic year, I spent a sabbatical year creating a Populism website,
which can be found at http://history.missouristate.edu/wrmiller/Populism/texts/
populism.htm. While the extensive bibliography has been the most used portion
of this website, I also included a forty-cartoon presentation on Populism.

Over the years I have gathered more than one thousand cartoons from Populist newspapers and employed Matt and several other students, most importantly Mariya C. Adams, to help clean them up. I am grateful for their efforts and also thank Dean Victor H. Matthews for providing an incentives grant to finance Mariya's work. I likewise thank another friend and colleague, James N. Giglio, for his encouragement and advice; I adopted the format he used in his *Truman in Cartoon and Caricature*. I also wish to thank Missouri State University for granting me a sabbatical leave for the 2008/2009 academic year to work on this project. Three other friends—Gregg Cantrell of Texas Christian University, Virgil Dean, editor of *Kansas History*, and James M. Beeby of Southern Indiana University—provided encouragement and invaluable information on anti-Populist cartoons. I also wish to thank staff at the Kansas Historical Society for permission to reprint cartoons they scanned from *Puck* and *Judge*.

Some of the ideas and phrases in this book appeared in some of my earlier publications. I thank Susan-Mary Grant, editor of *American Nineteenth Century History*, for permission to reproduce portions of "Educating the Masses: Cartoons from the Populist Press of the 1890s," which appeared in the summer 2003 issue, and Rowman & Littlefield Inc., for permission to reproduce portions of "Farmers and Third-Party Politics in Late Nineteenth-Century America," which appeared in *The Gilded Age: Perspectives on the Origins of Modern America*, edited by Charles W. Calhoun. Neither text is reproduced in its entirety, but in this book I have drawn liberally from both at various places.

This book aims to tell the story of the Populist Revolt through illustrations drawn from the Populist press of the 1890s. Because the object of cartoons is to evoke both an emotional and intellectual response, they frequently capture the spirit of their time better than written commentaries or historical essays, offering a window into the aspirations and concerns of both the illustrators and their readers. Thus, cartoons represent a valuable primary source from which we can gain insight into the world of the Populist Revolt a century ago. The cartoons presented in this book are from Populist newspapers of the 1890s, or in a few cases, from late 1880s newspapers committed to the proto-Populist Union Labor Party. Most were drawn originally for Populist publications; a few, however, first appeared in major daily newspapers and then were reprinted by Populist editors because they spoke to themes Populists could appreciate. Cross-pollination, of course, worked both ways. "The English Octopus: It Feeds on Nothing but Gold" (cartoon 4.26 in this book), for instance, appeared in the Populist-oriented *Republic County Freeman* on June 16, 1892. William H. "Coin" Harvey, a Democrat who was very popular among Populists, had the cartoon reprinted in his famous book, *Coin's Financial School*, which appeared in 1894. I have also included a few anti-Populist cartoons to give the reader some idea of how Populists fared in the mainstream press. Otherwise, all of the cartoons in this work came from newspapers committed to the People's Party.

Many of the cartoons in this book are from syndication pages that would have appeared in a number of newspapers at approximately the same date. Also, some Populist newspapers that regularly carried cartoons, such as the *American Nonconformist* (Winfield, KS, and Indianapolis, IN), *Representative* (St. Paul and Minneapolis, MN), and *Southern Mercury* (Dallas, TX), had regional and even national circulations; thus, their influence far exceeded the geographic scope of the newspaper's name. Although the cartoons in this book are mostly from Southwest, Plains, and Rocky Mountain states, they are broadly representative of Populist thinking as a whole. Examining the ideas emanating from Populist cartoons can provide insight into the course of the American republic in the late nineteenth century, in addition to illuminating some of the age-old concerns Americans have struggled with throughout our nation's history. My hope is that the illustrations will catch the eye of scholars and non-scholars alike, and that each will find the book both educational and entertaining.

Chapter 1

The Third-Party Tradition During the Gilded Age

THE BOISTEROUS WORLD OF GILDED AGE POLITICS climaxed and then abruptly ended with the Populist Revolt of the 1890s. During the late nineteenth century, voters of every ethnic and racial background, and from every walk of life, overwhelmingly participated in America's democratic experiment. Mainstream party politicians heralded the nation's institutions and gloried in their direction of the ship of state. By the mid-1890s, however, the angry intensity of the Populist Revolt threatened to undermine the establishment's right to set the nation's economic, social, and political agenda. In the caustic assessment of Republican newspaper editor William Allen White, these "ordinary clodhoppers...[who claim to] know more in a minute about finance than [ex-Treasury secretary] John Sherman," seemed on the verge of displacing the nation's contemporary elite.[1]

From the 1830s to the 1890s, political parties dominated American politics. Many voters believed that there were important ideological differences between the major parties. The Gilded Age Republican Party billed itself as the party of nationalism, prosperity, and moralism. Compared to its Democratic Party counterpart, the Grand Old Party (GOP) favored an activist, big government. It had saved the Union during the Civil War and Reconstruction, and it promoted a prosperous national economy through the protective tariff and pro-business subsidies. Because Republicans relied substantially upon the support of northern white Anglo-Saxon Protestants, it was the party of America's "host culture." Thus, the party often assumed the privilege of defining true Americanism and proper conduct, even to the point of imposing English language laws, prohibition

---

[1] Burnham, "Appearance and Disappearance of the American Voter," 44–46; McCormick, "Public Life in Industrial America," 95–96; and *Emporia Gazette* (KS), August 15, 1896. The editorial is reproduced in White, *Autobiography of William Allen White*, 281–82.

legislation, and blue laws. The Democratic Party, in contrast, was the party of Jeffersonian small government, noninterventionist laissez-faire economic policies, states' rights, and personal liberties. It endorsed the Jacksonian concept that government activism primarily helped the few at the expense of the many and that local government served the interests of citizens better than centralized national power. Democrats received most of their support from a diffuse range of ethnic and cultural "outgroups" that felt threatened by big government, such as recent immigrants and white southerners.[2]

The Populist Revolt of the 1890s was the culmination of two decades of third-party action that stretched back to the mid-1870s. With the end of Reconstruction in 1877, American politics settled into a period of political equilibrium, with the Democratic and Republican parties almost evenly matched throughout the period. While these two giants of American politics battled for national supremacy, fledgling third parties, like the Greenback (1876–78), Greenback-Labor (1880–86), Union Labor (1888), and People's or Populist (1890–1908) Parties, provided a significant alternative for dissatisfied voters. Populist newspapers and their cartoons played an important role in making the People's Party the largest and most important manifestation of late nineteenth-century third parties.

America's "first-past-the-post" electoral system (meaning whoever gets the most votes wins, even if the candidate received less than a majority) strongly encourages a two-party political system. The presence of third parties in American politics usually means one of the major parties has split and the other major party almost certainly will win. The losers usually recognize that the easiest way to regain power is to combine all opposition forces for the next election and work toward forming such a coalition. Thus, significant third parties, especially when they appear election after election, are quite unusual in American history.

The major third parties of the late nineteenth century provided just such an anomaly during the era that Mark Twain derisively labeled the "Gilded Age."[3] They died only to be reborn again almost instantly under a new name. There was a great deal of overlap in party leadership, platform proposals, and voters. James B. Weaver, for instance, was the Greenback-Labor candidate for president in 1880 and the Populist standard-bearer in 1892. Both the Union Labor Party of 1888 and People's Party of 1892 put forth platforms that emphasized a triumvirate of issues: land, transportation, and money. Both parties also inherited their monetary policies from the Greenback and Greenback-Labor Parties. These

---

[2] McCormick, "Party Period and Public Policy," 197–227; and Miller, "Lost World of Gilded Age Politics," 49–67.

[3] Mark Twain coined the phrase in his novel, *The Gilded Age: A Tale of Today,* which portrayed American society of the period as inordinately corrupt.

third parties prevented any candidate for president from receiving a majority of the popular votes from 1880 until 1896. Thus, they constituted a significant and continuing third-party presence in a political setting that strongly discouraged their existence.

Clearly, not all Americans were satisfied with the political scene of Gilded Age America. Voter turnout, however, was substantially higher than it is today. Gilded Age Americans were proud, and quite conscious, of their role as the vanguard of world republicanism. Only France, in 1871, had joined the ranks of republics in Europe. The rest of the world (save Latin America where American influence was strongest during the nineteenth century) was still ruled by some form of institutionalized privilege, usually a monarchy. Those dissatisfied with American politics during the Gilded Age, however, did not drop out of politics as the disaffected tend to do today. Instead, they tried to reform their major parties from within or joined third parties.

A major cause of dissatisfaction for many Americans was what they considered the inadequate response of both the Democratic and Republican parties to meeting the challenges produced by modernization. Rapid economic growth brought forth a revolutionary new America during the late nineteenth century. Industry expanded as never before. Railroad mileage grew fivefold between 1860 and 1890, making commercial agriculture possible in the West and upland South. Consequently, Americans brought 430 million new acres of land under cultivation between 1860 and 1900. The machinery that allowed American farmers to become the most efficient producers of the age also became widely available in this era. This reduced the time to produce twenty-seven different crops by 48 percent during the late nineteenth century. Thus, farmers found it desirable to buy machinery, fertilizer, and more land—all on credit.[4]

Despite these material advances, almost all historical accounts characterize the Gilded Age as a period in which farming went into decline. Farmers' share of the gross domestic product dropped from 38 percent in the 1870s to 24 percent in the 1890s. Millions lost their status as independent farmers and either became tenant farmers or joined the urban working poor in the nation's burgeoning factories. By the end of the century, a vocation championed by the nation's greatest public figures as the quintessence of Americanism was rapidly being swept away.[5] As the American farmer became a part of the world economy, the vagaries of feast or famine in Australia or the Ukraine also came to affect his life. His agricultural production vastly outpaced the capacity of the nation, and even the world, to purchase. Between 1870 and 1896, the wholesale price index for farm products

---

[4] McMath, *American Populism,* 20; and U.S. Bureau of the Census, *Historical Statistics of the United States,* 141, 278, 427.

[5] Shannon, *Farmer's Last Frontier,* 135–36, 144.

declined by 50 percent, but railroads and other middlemen took their profits despite the farmer's plight. Critics complained that farmers had overproduced. Farmers who lived in a world of underclothed and underfed people considered this nonsense. With an equitable distribution of wealth, everyone would have the purchasing power to buy farmers' products.[6]

These farmers and laborers constituted the largest elements of the Populist following. They found both the demagoguery of reviving Civil War animosities and the major parties' ritual battles over tariff protection to be purposeful misdirections from seeking solutions to the nation's real problems: the widening gap between rich and poor, monetary deflation that brought falling commodity prices, farm and shop bankruptcies, and the proletarianization of urban laborers. Over the previous thirty years, government had promoted railroad expansion with land grant subsidies, industry with the protective tariff, and finance with favorable banking and currency legislation. The result was monopolistic practices by those interests that hurt small producers. Farmers were being driven off the land. Factory and mine conditions were horrific. The nation's social and economic elite promoted ideas like social Darwinism to justify such trends as the price of progress. For Populists, these ideas threatened to destroy the egalitarian promise of America; no one had migrated to the United States to become a landless peasant.

It fell to the Southern Farmers' Alliance to respond to this degeneration from republican equality. Benjamin Clover, the president of the Kansas branch of the Alliance, spoke for those who would become Populists when he told them that "it is just as essential for you to send men of your own kind to represent you as it is for you to go out and cultivate your own crops."[7] No farmer or laborer expected a lawyer or merchant to help him in his fields or workshop; why should they expect them to represent the producers' interests in government? Replacing the political elite with true representatives of the people is a theme common to all so-called populist movements.

Local Populist parties began to appear in Kansas in 1889 and culminated in the founding of the national People's Party in July 1892. The third party's heyday, however, stretched from its first statewide victory in the 1890 Kansas legislative races to the People's Party becoming a coalition partner of the Democratic Party in 1896. Between those dates, Populists posed a serious challenge to the mainstream party direction of the nation. The issues they agitated for are still relevant today.

---

[6] Morgan, *History of the Wheel and Alliance,* 511–18; and U.S. Census Bureau, *Historical Statistics of the United States,* 115, 117.

[7] *Territorial Topic* (Purcell, Chickasaw Nation), June 5, 1890.

A major weapon in the arsenal of the upstart Populist Party was what they called "education." Reform editors held the conviction that the first step toward correcting the evils that corrupted American society was knowledge. Justice would then come from a politically empowered producer class. The mainstream party press exercised an information monopoly that, according to Populists, they used as a "vehicle for the conveyance of plutocratic [monopolistic] ideas to the public." Therefore, the primary function of the mainstream press was to "conceal the truth" from the public.[8] Producers needed an alternative source of information that was honest and spoke directly to their interests. As Julius Wayland, editor of the *Appeal to Reason* (Kansas City), put it in 1896, "education is needed more than offices.... When education has done its necessary work, the offices will follow to enforce the wishes of the people. Offices without education will do more harm than good."[9]

As a party of poor people, the Populist Party needed both a strong grassroots organization and an inexpensive means of communication to educate potential followers and rally them to the cause. The Southern Farmers' Alliance provided both until its collapse around 1892. It was far larger than the Grange, which had fed into the Greenback and Greenback-Labor parties, or the Knights of Labor, which spawned the Union Labor Party. Reform-oriented newspapers, which grew in numbers throughout the 1890s, filled the void afterward. It was the Alliance and reform editors, plus a severe downturn of the economy in the 1890s, that made the People's Party the most important third-party effort in this era.

Because it only took about $100 ($2,357 in 2009 dollars) to establish a small newspaper during the 1890s, many localities had two or three. Most were political in their orientation and highly partisan. Such newspapers could be potent political weapons because of their media monopoly in the days before radio and television. Only the stump speaker and book author rivaled them. Because party propaganda was the major function of Populist papers, their editors accepted both cash and produce in payment and rarely cut off a subscriber for nonpayment. To encourage subscriptions, most offered package deals whereby their subscribers could receive one of the popular reform books of the day or another Populist newspaper at a discount.

Not only did the reform press educate the masses and inform the faithful, it also provided a valuable legitimizing function. Mainstream sources heaped ridicule upon farmer and laborer ideas. They determined which events were newsworthy and which seemed eccentric. Populist editors defended reform with

---

[8] *Alva Review* (Oklahoma Territory), April 25, 1895; and Mitchell, *Political Education,* 100.

[9] *Appeal to Reason* (Kansas City), July 18, 1896. After the collapse of the Populist movement in 1896, the *Appeal to Reason* relocated to Girard, Kansas, where it became the nation's leading socialist newspaper with nationwide circulation.

stories of farm troubles and mistreatment of laborers that gained sympathy for the movement. Frequently, Populist editors covered stories of interest to producers more extensively and more accurately than their mainstream counterparts, who had little knowledge of, or even interest in, hinterland conditions. Reform editors also provided statements by authoritative figures who made the movement seem reasonable, competent, and progressive, instead of naïve, unsophisticated, and ignorant, as the mainstream press insisted.[10]

Reform editors made little distinction between hard news and editorial opinion. This was consistent with contemporary rural press ethical standards.[11] Poses of impartiality and objectivity are almost never the tools of dissenters.[12] Bluntly rejecting the status quo is necessary to building a reform movement. To do this, the National Reform Press Association (NRPA), which the Southern Farmers' Alliance founded in 1890, provided coordination of efforts in addition to "ready-print" editorials that many affiliates reproduced. The NRPA claimed more than one thousand affiliate papers in the 1890s. Alabama, Georgia, Kansas, and Texas each had more than one hundred.[13]

The vast majority of Populist newspapers appeared weekly. Some of the larger, more important journals were run quite professionally. Many small-town weeklies, however, had a more amateurish quality about them. Secondhand printing presses typeset with faded or broken letters abounded. The smallest papers consisted of a large sheet of paper folded from side to side and printed on both sides to form a four-page newspaper. At least one of these pages would have quite a superior appearance compared to the others. This was provided by one of the Populist Party's "boilerplate" syndication services. It contained national news, party propaganda, and frequently a cartoon. Because many larger Populist papers also carried these syndications, they constituted a relatively uniform source of political information for readers. Political scientist Roscoe Martin claimed that it was "almost as if the party had published one great paper." He estimated that only one-quarter of Texas' reform editors were professional journalists, and historian Seymour Lutzky found the same percentage in the Midwest. Most editors

---

[10] Folkerts, "Functions of the Reform Press," 23–24.

[11] Lutzky, "Reform Editors," 54.

[12] Shoemaker, "Perceived Legitimacy of Deviant Political Groups," 249–85.

[13] Lutzky, "Reform Editors," 13; Fischer, *Them Damned Pictures*, 31–32; Martin, *People's Party in Texas*, 189, 202n; Hicks, *Populist Revolt*, 131; *Oklahoma Representative* (Guthrie), March 26, 1896; and Goodwyn, *Populist Moment*, 116. The *American Newspaper Annual* contains significant information (such as the names of editors, political affiliations, numbers of subscriptions, etc.) on newspapers during the Populist era. It began publication in 1880 and, although the name has changed a bit over the years, is still in publication today. The exact number of Populist-affiliated newspapers cannot be determined with any great accuracy. Some were in business for only a brief period. One contemporary source claimed 187 reform papers for Texas and 174 for Kansas. See *Oklahoma Representative* (Guthrie), February 27, 1896; and Goodwyn, *Populist Moment*, 206.

were in their thirties, and they frequently dominated local and/or state Populist executive committees. Party growth was crucial to increasing subscription, and publishing only once a week left them more time for party duties than farmers or laborers typically had available. Thus, the reform editors who ran the illustrations presented in this book served as a vital link between third-party officeholders and the party's rank and file.[14]

Modern scholars are not totally convinced that cartoons change minds. Twentieth-century cartoonist Pat Oliphant claims that cartoons "at best precipitate thought and dialogue."[15] Historian Charles Press has argued that people frequently have plenty of information; what they want is someone they trust to interpret the information for them.[16] Providing interpretations that countered the conventional wisdom of the mainstream press and politicians was a vital part of the educational process of the Populist press. Third-party editors, however, clearly saw cartoons as a recruitment tool. Their role was to make a connection with potential recruits and lure them away from the mainstream parties. Democratic and Republican party editors in the South and West, where Populists were strongest, were far less likely to run illustrations than their Populist rivals. They already had an established clientele, and experience told them that recruitment from other parties was unlikely. Thus, Populist editors had to go the extra mile to build a following. Regularly publishing political cartoons was a major part of this effort. Their success in finding recruits suggests Populist cartoons accurately reflected the values, beliefs, and even prejudices of the Populist rank and file.

In many ways, the cartoonists of the Populist movement were political assassins (figuratively, of course) with artistic talent. Harpooning plutocrats was their vocation. Only three appear to have held steady work as cartoonists. Chicago artist Andrew V. Ullmark, a Swedish immigrant, regularly drew cartoons for the National Reform Press Association's ready-print service based in St. Louis. Ullmark apparently had a contract with W. Scott Morgan, editor of the NRPA's syndications, for the illustrations.

Roger Cunningham was a pioneer in photoengraving. He was born in 1853 in rural New York, but moved to Kansas in his midteens. Cunningham became the youngest editor in Kansas in 1875, but moved on to Chicago in 1879, where he took up wood and wax engraving of images. Shortly afterward he began to work with photoengraving. Cunningham moved to Toronto to teach engraving processes in 1885; he was renowned for his chemical and technical expertise. In

---

[14] Martin, *People's Party in Texas,* 194, 198, 201; and Lutzky, "Reform Editors," 14–15, 28. A. N. Kellogg, who invented boilerplate syndication, provided materials to Democrats, Republicans, and Populists in the 1890s.

[15] Fischer, *Them Damned Pictures,* 14–15.

[16] Press, *Political Cartoon,* 50–51.

1888, Cunningham took charge of the A. N. Kellogg Newspaper Co. branch in Kansas City, where he produced the cartoons that appear in this work. Kellogg also provided ready-print syndications for Democratic- and Republican-oriented papers throughout the Midwest from its Chicago plant. Teachenor-Bartberger Engraving Co. bought Kellogg's Kansas City facilities in 1893 and made Cunningham a partner. Later in life, Cunningham worked as an oil and watercolor artist. The Smithsonian Institution, Pratt Institute of Technology, and Boston Museum of Fine Arts displayed his work in their graphic arts sections.[17]

The third regularly employed Populist cartoonist was Wilbur Steele of the *Rocky Mountain News* (Denver, CO), one of the few Populist daily newspapers. Steele was born in Illinois, but grew up in California. After bouncing around from job to job as a young man landed him in Denver, John Adkins, proprietor of the *Rocky Mountain News,* caught a glimpse of some of Steele's sketches and hired him to draw cartoons for his paper. Steele had been developing his artistic talents as a hobby for years, but his encounter with Adkins occurred at exactly the time when newspapers began to run cartoons regularly. Thus, he got into the profession at its very inception. Because his wife's family was in the newspaper business, Steele understood the journalistic needs of his new employer from the very beginning. A cartoonist's illustrations quickly made him the unofficial mouthpiece for his publication; accordingly, he had to maintain a close working relationship with his editor to keep his job.[18]

The rest of the Populist cartoonists, including the best and most famous, Watson Heston of Carthage, Missouri, worked freelance. Heston was a photographer by trade and was best noted for his illustrations for the freethinker journal *Truth Seeker* (New York), many of which were later published in *The Old Testament Comically Illustrated* (1890), *The New Testament Comically Illustrated* (1898), and *The Bible Comically Illustrated* (1900).[19] Heston only occasionally used religious themes in his Populist cartoons. He was the only cartoonist recognized in the 1896 Populist convention's official program.[20]

Heston, like other cartoonists, sometimes drafted illustrations of his own conception. Other times he received commissions to draft cartoons to editors' specifications.[21] Where did Heston stand among the great cartoonists of his day? Probably nowhere. Both physically and intellectually, he labored outside the mainstream. It is doubtful that he cared what other illustrators thought of his

---

[17] Ward and Ward, *Process Photogram,* 40, 172.

[18] Bonner, "History of Illustration Among America's Major Newspapers."

[19] Because of the blasphemous nature of these books, few have survived.

[20] *Official Souvenir of the National Convention of the People's Party at St. Louis; Jasper County Democrat* (Carthage, MO), January 31, 1905; *Carthage Weekly Press* (MO), February 2, 1905; and *Truth Seeker* (New York), March 4, 1905.

[21] Lutzky, "Reform Editors," 60.

work. His peer group was full of Populists and freethinkers, not big-city cartoon-ists. The editor of the *Truth Seeker* once offered to bring him to New York City for formal training. Heston declined. Like many Populist cartoonists, he was more ideologically driven than big-city illustrators whose livelihood depended upon serving editors who might have differing political views from the artist. Such people had nothing to teach Heston that he valued.[22]

Ready-print pages and regularly appearing cartoons were relatively new developments during the late nineteenth century. The processes that made such items available to editors reduced the cost of production to the point where it greatly democratized the profession of journalism. Inexpensive, country, and small-town newspapers thus became an ideal medium for empowering a grass-roots movement of poor people, like Populism.

Ansel Nash Kellogg, a Wisconsin country editor with a Columbia Univer-sity education, was the first newspaperman to successfully use ready-print mate-rials.[23] At the beginning of the American Civil War in 1861, editors like Kellogg found themselves short of manpower, especially typesetters. Kellogg contracted with a Madison daily newspaper to print one side of his paper on their newer, faster printing presses. This saved Kellogg time and money. It also provided his readers with fresher dispatches from the war front and news of the world. Other country editors followed suit. At the end of the war, Kellogg sold his paper, moved to Chicago, and began his own ready-print service. Because Kellogg made his ready-print pages anonymous, his product made many of his editor-customers appear to be more skilled than they actually were. Until the great Chicago fire of 1871 disrupted production, most readers did not even know about the ready-print business. By that time, Kellogg had a circulation of more than 140,000 readers. Because most local newspapers were highly partisan, Kellogg produced different pages for Democratic and Republican newspapers. By the time Kellogg passed away in 1886, there were four major and numerous minor ready-print services in America.[24]

Kellogg died about the time cartoons became a regular feature of news-papers. In the eighteenth century, editors used woodcuts to reproduce images for their papers and magazines. Woodcuts were difficult and time-consuming to make, but wood could stand up to long pressruns better than other materials of the day. On the other hand, they needed to be cut to size as a mirror image of the illustration to be published. A new process, lithography, where an artist drew an

[22] *Truth Seeker* (New York), March 4, 1905.

[23] Although the terms "ready-print" and "boilerplate" originally had different meanings (the former being printed by a syndication service and the latter being the metal or papier-mâché printed plates sent to the newspaper for local printing), both terms had roughly the same meanings by the 1890s.

[24] Harter, *Boilerplating America*, 17–22.

image on limestone with a grease pencil and then rolled ink on it to produce a print, emerged in the 1790s. Lithography, however, did not solve the problems of size or of drawing a mirror image of the illustration. America's struggling weekly magazines stuck to the cheaper woodcuts before the mid-1850s. Both lithography and wood engraving permitted reproduction of a cartoon within two or three days of the artist's final rendering of an illustration. In the meantime, the London *Times* was the first newspaper to replace its handpress with one driven by steam in 1815. These developments set the stage for the mass production of political art.

Thomas Nast became America's first great cartoonist, drawing rather overblown panoramas for *Harpers Weekly* magazine during the American Civil War. Nast simplified his style after the war, which elevated his work to legendary heights. He invented the donkey and the elephant as symbols of the Democratic and Republican parties. Nast's success encouraged others to follow. Joseph Keppler founded *Puck,* a humor magazine that regularly ran cartoons in 1877, soon followed by *Judge* in 1881 and *Life* in 1883.

One last technological advance made the daily editorial cartoon a possibility for almost all newspapers: photoengraving. This new process allowed illustrations to be drawn frontwards and to reduce or enlarge them as needed. Presses could reproduce such cartoons only an hour or two after the cartoonist had finished his work. Joseph Pulitzer's *New York World* was the first to run cartoons as a regular feature in 1884. Others quickly followed. With the availability of readyprint services, even the smallest papers could run illustrations as a regular feature by the late 1880s.[25]

Exaggeration and stereotyping are time-honored staples of cartoons, frequently capturing the underlying truth of a situation better than the written word. They also left a more lasting impression upon the reader than an editorial and could reach those whose reading skills were below par. The cartoons that appeared in Populist newspapers must have struck a significant chord with their readers, as such illustrations had to be purchased and most Populist newspapers were run on a shoestring budget. It was a chord that has touched the soul of American politics ever since, as evidenced by the continued use of the word "populist" to denote a person, group, or idea at odds with a perceived elite.[26]

---

[25] Press, *Political Cartoon,* 43–47.

[26] Fischer, *Them Damned Pictures,* xiii; and Mitchell, *Political Education,* 100.

1.1: "People's Party Gains"
Source: *Kansas Populist* (Cherryvale), April 20, 1894.

This is a typical Populist "ready-print" syndication from the National Reform Press Association in St. Louis, which included national news, party propaganda, and a cartoon. Andrew V. Ullmark, a Chicago artist who produced most of the NRPA's illustrations, drew this cartoon. The distributor would mail the local newspaper a papier-mâché plate that editors could cut into strips that would fit their paper's particular needs or, as in this case, publish the page as a whole.

Chapter 2

The Populist Critique of Gilded Age America

POPULISTS DREW FROM A VARIETY OF INTELLECTUAL SOURCES, both modern and traditional, in their attempt to understand the economic, political, and social convulsions that characterized the last quarter of the nineteenth century. The most important influence was what modern historians have labeled "the republicanism of the American Revolution." It was from this source that Americans have drawn their commitment to republicanism (as opposed to monarchy), democracy, liberty, and equality. Thus, the Populist Revolt was a thoroughly American response to Gilded Age development.[1] Nineteenth-century Americans were very conscious of the fact that the United States, as the first modern republic, represented the vanguard of republicanism throughout the world, and America's leadership in promoting republicanism was duly recognized. During the American Civil War, for instance, British mill workers suffered from the Union blockade that cut off the export of cotton to Britain. Still, they viewed the South's slave society and "Cavalier ethic" as unacceptably aristocratic, and eagerly expressed support for the Union over the Confederate States of America.[2]

Republicanism defined the original meaning of the American republic. When the Founding Fathers believed that King George III had conspired to subvert their liberties and impose England's static social and economic system upon the colonies, they revolted and formed a republic. Establishing a republic at a time when all other modern nations were ruled by some form of institutionalized privilege committed the United States to the concept of equality. In keeping with this commitment, early Americans expressed profound disapproval of government favors to banking elites and aid to monopolies, the widening gap between

---

[1] For more on the development of the concept of republicanism, see Shalhope, "Toward a Republican Synthesis," 49–80.

[2] McPherson, *Battle Cry of Freedom,* 549.

rich and poor, and driving farmers off the land into dependent subservience, policies that had defined English development throughout most of the eighteenth
century. Many colonists had shouldered the burdens of interoceanic migration
to escape the lack of opportunity afforded the poor and middling elements of
the Old World, an area most nineteenth-century Americans still associated with
poverty and oppression. The great threat to the American way of life before 1917
was monarchy. Only when World War I destroyed monarchy and Russia fell to
the Communists with the Bolshevik Revolution did this change.

Most late eighteenth- and nineteenth-century Americans viewed the British
political system as particularly corrupt, a view that dated back to the emergence
of Sir Robert Walpole as Britain's first prime minister in 1720. Walpole stabilized
the turbulent British political system by building majorities and silencing critics through the liberal use of patronage, pensions, and franchises. Walpole and
his successors then financed their manipulations through bonding schemes that
rewarded insiders and saddled future generations with a seemingly impossible
debt. By the 1770s, American colonists had come to the conclusion that corruption had so totally subverted Britain's political system that separation from the
mother country was the only way to retain their liberties. The American Revolution constituted a rejection of this corrupt system and institutionalized the values of republicanism, equality, and liberty. After the Revolution, Americans saw
Britain's political system as a prime example of what must be avoided in order to
retain American liberties. Even a century later, most Americans, and especially
Populists, expressed the most profound Anglophobia.

Many Gilded Age Americans considered the lessons handed down from
the Founding Fathers to be universal truths, valid for all times and conditions.
To Populists, Britain represented the unacceptable gap between rich and poor
that unfairly destined the few to the privileges of aristocracy and the many to
dependency and destitution. Populists viewed late nineteenth-century America's widening class distinctions, government-sponsored promotion of economic
development, expanding bureaucracies, and pro-business financial policies as
thinly disguised attempts to turn America from its democratic heritage into a
European-style autocracy. Thus, Populists liberally applied the terms "robber
baron" and "cattle baron" to those who seemingly had gotten so far ahead economically as to constitute an American pseudo-aristocracy.[3]

As with the Founding Fathers, Populists viewed the public world as separated
into two antagonistic spheres: power and liberty. This usually meant governmental power and individual liberty. Power was believed to be ever aggressive in its

---

[3] Shalhope, *Roots of Democracy,* 42. Men who would later become Populists apparently invented the
terms "robber baron" and "cattle baron" (or at least their modern usage) in the 1880s. See Miller, *Oklahoma
Populism,* 220n.

desire to take away people's liberties. This required those who wished to retain their liberties to be ever vigilant and jealous of their liberties. Such a view led people to expect alternating periods of progress and decay in society as the forces of governmental power and individual liberty struggled for ascendancy. Only an egalitarian society with widespread property ownership could ensure that none would be so strong as to be able to misuse power and none so weak as to be unable to withstand the encroachments of those wielding power.[4]

The cyclical interpretation of social development that Populists inherited lent positive connotations to the simplicity, equality, industriousness, and frugality of a developing society and a negative attitude to the hedonism, luxury, venality, and exploitation of a developed nation. The latter constituted a triumph of the forces of power over liberty. This humanistic orientation was moral in nature and dictated the rejection of any social development that encouraged human debasement. Such a viewpoint naturally had special appeal to those who saw themselves as victims of the contemporary trends of late nineteenth-century America.[5]

Whether the course of late nineteenth-century American development constituted an advance of civilization or a degeneration toward barbarism became a major point of contention with the coming of the Populist Revolt of the 1890s. Some Americans pointed to material factors, such as increased wealth, expanded production, and a proliferation of services, as signs of the nation's advance. The plight of individual victims (such as indebted farmers and injured factory workers) was a small price to pay for what they labeled progress. Others noted similarities with inherited warnings of social degeneration from the Founding Fathers. Gilded Age lawmakers, for instance, seemed to abdicate their responsibility for monetary policy to America's and, worse yet, England's banker elite. The protective tariff and land grants to railroads promoted the ultimate consolidation of wealth and power: monopoly. The gap between the rich and the poor widened distinctly in late nineteenth-century America, and the bulwark of liberty in a republic—the independent family farmer—appeared to suffer the most. Farm foreclosures were endemic by the 1890s. Most aggravating, recent intellectual currents like social Darwinism argued that such victims deserved their fate because of their inherent inferiority. America's social and economic elite seemed visibly impressed with such an interpretation. Because social Darwinism came to America from Britain, Populists viewed it as an alien ideology, and a treasonous betrayal of the original meaning of America.

In an Independence Day 1889 address entitled "Objects of the Alliance," Benjamin Clover, president of the Kansas branch of the proto-Populist Southern Farmers' Alliance, made clear the orientation of his order. He called upon

[4] Shalhope, *Roots of Democracy*, 43.
[5] Ibid., 44–45.

Alliancemen to "close up the ranks, stand shoulder to shoulder, and clear the decks of all old hindering prejudices, party strifes, or sectional animosities…[to save] the America, given into our keeping by the Revolutionary Fathers." Farmers and laborers, he continued, were all that stood between the "monarchy of wealth, on the one hand, and the anarchy of poverty, on the other."[6] Most Populists were thoroughly convinced that great concentrations of wealth not only impoverished millions, but also bred radical responses to that unfairness, such as anarchism.

To millions of Gilded Age Americans, farming was a way of life that was infused with honor and patriotism. When the revolutionary fathers turned their attention to the problem of how to retain their liberties, they envisioned a republican government supported by an independent citizenry as the best safeguard. Individual economic independence was necessary to withstand the temptations and threats of those with power. Because independent farmers constituted the rock upon which the republic stood, Americans had developed a freehold concept consistent with the advancement of small farmer interests.[7] The social and economic trends of America by the 1890s appeared to be taking the nation in a very different, more exploitative, direction.

The concept of a classless, egalitarian society based upon the virtues of the morally invigorated freeholder influenced American thought throughout the nineteenth century. Such a world was possible only if those who labored with their hands were the ones to benefit from the wealth they produced. In the view of Populists, middlemen, speculators, bankers, and other exploiters had obtained their wealth illegitimately through manipulation. So long as labor was the only legitimate source of wealth, America would remain a classless society. No man could perform enough labor to greatly widen the gap over others who worked with their hands. Only those who exploited producers through manipulation could destroy the American dream of an egalitarian society.

Populist cartoonists employed a number of methods to create negative impressions of what they considered to be illegitimate financial interests. Wall Street has retained its connotations of corporate greed in the twenty-first century. John Bull, a symbol of British arrogance, wearing a suit and top hat and frequently carrying a bag of money in his hand, was one of the symbols Populist cartoonists used to depict the British finance industry. It had the added advantage of feeding Populist Anglophobia. The other major symbol of financial interests that some Populist cartoonists employed was the Jewish moneylender, Shylock. Occasionally, the Shylock image would be labeled Rothschild, the name of a famous Jewish banking family that Queen Victoria elevated to the English nobility in 1885.

---

[6] *American Nonconformist* and *Kansas Industrial Liberator* (Winfield, KS), July 4, 1889.

[7] Smith, *Virgin Land*, 41.

In light of the career of Adolph Hitler, it is very difficult to interpret anti-Semitic cartoons today as they might have been understood by people in the 1890s. The Nazi mass murder of six million Jews has forever made western society more sensitive to ethnic and racial stereotyping. But reducing complex economic, political, and social issues to visual shorthand is a necessary part of the cartoonist's trade. Rather than invent such images, it was often easier, and more effective, to rely upon already existing formulas that impart a meaning that would take volumes to explain in words. Shylock filled the Populist cartoonist's need for an easily recognizable villain representing heartless greed, cunning, and lack of scruples.[8] This image of Shylock originally emerged from the unsympathetic, even hostile, Christian milieu of Europe centuries before the Populist Revolt, and *Puck*, *Judge*, and *Life* had already employed such images in the late nineteenth century. This made Shylock a familiar and acceptable figure to many contemporary Americans. The American version of Shylock also had northeastern, urban, and capitalist connotations for Populists.[9] The fact that Jewish stereotyping also conjured up images of the alien who refused to fully assimilate (as most Americans expect immigrants to do) raises ethnic and religious concerns for Americans today.

Caricatures frequently are not based upon the close observation of real people. Populist use of the Shylock figure was imitative. As a threatening figure, Shylock could be drawn in as vicious a manner as the artist's talent would allow. Populist cartoonists wasted little sympathy on other threatening figures like Grover Cleveland, John Sherman, or John Bull. Perhaps third-party cartoonists felt less inhibition in using the Shylock image because Populist country had few Jews who might be offended; on the other hand, proximity to significant Jewish populations did not appear to restrain anti-Populist publications like *Puck*, *Judge*, or *Life*.

A variety of scholars have debated exactly what the Shylock image conjured up in the minds of pre–Nazi-era Americans. Historian Oscar Handlin has even contended that Jewish stereotypes "were not meant and not taken" as anti-Semitic insults.[10] Most Americans were insensitive to how much ethnic stereotypes could be hurtful. Ethnic humor was common in such a diverse nation, and only occasionally did late nineteenth-century Jews publicly complain about ethnically charged cartoons.[11] Jews were not the only ethnic or racial group to be targeted by negative ethnic stereotypes nor did they receive the most vicious treatment. That was reserved for the Irish, Chinese, and African Americans. Other scholars,

---

[8] Appel, "Jews in American Caricature," 107–9.

[9] Glanz, *Jew in Early American Wit and Graphic Humor,* 227.

[10] Handlin, "American Views of the Jew," 328.

[11] Appel, "Jews in American Caricature," 117.

like Michael Dobkowski, believe such interpretations of the meaning and extent of anti-Semitism are unduly benign.[12]

To put Populist anti-Semitism in perspective, C. Vann Woodward noted that fourteen Jewish societies in Brooklyn formally protested in 1899 that "no Jew can go on the street without exposing himself to the danger of being pitilessly beaten." His point was that anti-Semitism was everywhere, and probably more threatening in the ethnically diverse Northeast than in Populist country. Even such a critic of Populism as New Yorker Richard Hofstadter has argued that Populist anti-Semitism was entirely verbal and rhetorical.[13]

Only two Populist cartoonists—Watson Heston and Carl Browne—extensively used the Shylock figure. Heston's work appeared in numerous third-party newspapers, including Henry and Leo Vincent's *American Nonconformist*, Jacob Coxey's *Sound Money*, and Ignatius Donnelly's *The Representative*, all of whom were major players in the Populist Revolt. Browne, who was Coxey's son-in-law, published almost exclusively in *Sound Money*. Some of the most important Populist sources of communication with the masses did not shy away from the ethnic stereotyping that was common in their day, so obviously their clientele was not deeply offended. Did they consider Shylock to be no more than a metaphor for financial excess or did the image impart a strong ethnic prejudice as well? Perhaps we will never be able to determine the relative degrees of insensitivity and malice Populist anti-Semitic cartoons were meant to project, but ethnic malice does not appear to dominate.

---

[12] Dobkowski, *Tarnished Dream*, 5–7.

[13] Woodward, "Populist Heritage and the Intellectual," 154–55; and Hofstadter, *Age of Reform*, 80.

"GET OFF, AND BLEED YOUR SELVES A WHILE. LIBERTY I MUST HAVE--I GIVE YOU FAIR WARNING."

2.1: "Get Off and Bleed Yourselves a While"
Source: *American Nonconformist* (Winfield, KS), July 16, 1891.

Populists' major complaint was that politicians and Wall Street held "the people" down by manipulating the political system. This problem could be solved only by a "rising of the people" that would restore popular control of government. In this illustration, "the people" are represented as Jonathan Swift's fictional character Gulliver and various interests (Wall Street, Democratic and Republican parties, and monopoly) appear as petty, but vicious, Lilliputians.

Many Populist cartoons showed quite a bit of detail. The label to the palette on which Gulliver is tied, for instance, reads "National Democratic-Republican Platform." Populists contended that there was no difference between the mainstream parties. The Tompkins Square Heroes sign (bottom left) refers to an 1874 New York City labor demonstration broken up by the police. Tom Scott (bottom right) was the long-time president of the Pennsylvania Central Railroad and mentor to industrialist Andrew Carnegie.

WE ARE STILL HIS SUBJECTS.

So long as the United States lives under the English Gold System, just so long do American Producers remain the slaves of British Imperialism. Let us shake off the British yoke (Gold) once more by establishing a currency (Silver) the basis of supply of which is not in British possessions.—People's Party.

2.2: "We Are Still His Subjects"
Source: *Anthony Weekly Bulletin* (KS), June 22, 1894.

Populists complained that America had not sufficiently distanced itself from British domination since the American Revolution. Wall Street and pro-English banking policies, namely the gold standard, kept the United States in vassalage to the British. Here John Bull (Britain's Uncle Sam) drives a chariot labeled "American nation" that tramples Columbia. President Grover Cleveland takes a backseat to John Bull, who is in control of the team driving the nation. Britain set the standards of international trade in the nineteenth century, very much as the United States does today. By demanding gold in international trade, Britain forced the United States onto the gold standard in 1873, which caused massive deflation in America. Adoption of the gold standard especially hurt farmers and silver miners. As in this illustration, Populist cartoonists used the John Bull figure to symbolize Old World aggression, autocracy, and unfairness, which were treasonous to the American republican tradition.

WASHINGTON'S PROPHECY FULFILLED.

GEORGE WASHINGTON (Farewell Address).—"We should look to the future: for a power not of the people (plutocracy) may seek to destroy this free government. Eternal vigilance is the price of liberty."
THOMAS JEFFERSON (Democrat 1801).—"All men being created free and equal, it is therefore a fundamental principle of this government to guarantee equal rights to all and special priviledge to none."
ABRAHAM LINCOLN (Republican 1860).—"A government by the people, for the people and of the people shall not perish from the earth."
PLUTOCRACY (1896).—"Them fellows were foolish to believe that they could keep me off this throne."

2.3: "Washington's Prophecy Fulfilled"
Source: *Anthony Weekly Bulletin* (KS), March 30, 1894.

Populists invoke the warnings of their greatest heroes, Washington, Jefferson, and Lincoln, about the degeneration from republican equality to monopolistic privilege that they saw in late nineteenth-century America. Monarchy, aristocracy, and other forms of privilege constituted a negative counterimage to American republicanism. Populist editors and cartoonists loved to quote from the Founding Fathers. In doing so, they defended the original meaning of America as a place where relatively equal small producers dominated. They were particularly incensed at the greed and exploitation implicit in the reigning ideologies of social Darwinism, laissez-faire capitalism, and the gospel of wealth, and saw the growing wealth, power, and aristocratic pretensions of America's corporate interests as a subversion of American republicanism.

IS THIS NATION A BRITISH DEPENDENCY?

Why should the United States the greatest silver producing nation in the world, humbly beg England and Germany for permission to coin her silver into money? The United States could maintain silver upon a parity with gold, at a ratio of 16 to 1 in spite of the entire world.

2.4: "Is This Nation a British Dependency?"
Source: *Republic County Freeman* (Belleville, KS), July 7, 1892.

Columbia turns away in shame as a rather frail Uncle Sam bows down in subservience to John Bull and Queen Victoria of England. Both the Democratic and Republican parties tried to straddle the money issue because it divided their parties. This illustration quotes from the Republican Party platform of 1892, which calls for an international conference to adopt bimetallism (silver and gold) as the standard for international trade. Populists claimed this was a subterfuge for supporting the gold standard. Neither Britain nor Germany would ever consent to an international conference designed to include silver. In the meantime, silver mines and wheat farmers suffer. Notice the British throne and the snooty expressions on John Bull and Queen Victoria's faces. The cartoonist portrays support for Populism as the patriotic choice for true Americans.

THE TORY IS STILL HERE.

UNCLE SAM—*That* fellow is just the same as he used to be and I'll have to give him another dose of the same medicine. It was an international disagreement and not an international agreement that I started with. I need another disagreement pretty badly in my business right now. I'm going to have it.

2.5: "The Tory is Still Here"
Source: *Rocky Mountain News* (Denver, CO), June 16, 1895.

Populists applied the term "goldbug" to supporters of the gold standard. They argued that it was a pro-British policy. Tories (Americans who remained loyal to the British crown during the American Revolution) were considered traitors to the American republican tradition. In this cartoon by A. W. (Wilbur) Steele, a well-dressed goldbug prays to John Bull who sits atop a pillow labeled "Sound Money" (a euphemism for the gold standard) with the British flag draped in front of him. The year 1778 was a turning point for the American Revolution; Americans defeated a major British army at the Battle of Saratoga, which brought France into the war on the side of the colonists, a crucial factor in the ultimate American victory.

FRUITS OF AMERICAN PLUTOCRACY.

American Millionaire—So, Duke, you want my daughter's hand in marriage?
The Duke—I would give name and honor through her hand.
   American Millionaire —Have you scrofula? Are you dissipated? In other words, have you all the contaminations common to noble blood?
   The Duke—I'm afflicted with scrofula, epilepsy; am dissipated, disreputable, and a scoundrel.
   American Millionaire—Take her, then, and may heaven bless my children.   —With apologies to Texas Siftings.

2.6: "Fruits of American Plutocracy"
Source: *Anthony Weekly Bulletin* (KS), November 15, 1895.

As the gap between rich and poor widened in late nineteenth-century America, Populists believed that the newly rich aspired to aristocratic status. This cartoon pokes fun at the American robber baron's excitement over his daughter's marriage to European nobility. The cartoonist's purpose is to associate American millionaires with a degeneration from American vigor and wholesomeness into European effeteness and dissipation. Americans communed with nature by working the land, while overdevelopment removed Europeans from the morally invigorating effects of nature. This was a common theme of American identity during the nineteenth century.

King Grover I. and a Pair of His Most Devoted Subjects.

2.7: "King Grover I, and a Pair of His Most Devoted Subjects"
Source: *Kansas Populist* (Cherryvale), January 5, 1894.

President Grover Cleveland (1885–89 and 1893–97) took much of the blame for bad economic times of the 1890s. His financial policies (especially in promoting the gold standard) seemed pro-British and thus aristocratic. In this cartoon, a politician and Wall Street beseech King Grover I for special favors.

Populists believed that America's economic elite obtained their position not through honest labor, but by securing illegitimate government aid. "In hoc signo vinces" (with this as your standard you shall have victory) was the motto of Roman Emperor Constantine. He had adopted the Christian cross as his standard for the Battle of the Milvian Bridge, the battle that made him emperor. Cleveland's cross, however, is the gold standard, which has brought him rather poor popular support.

THE KING BUSINESS.

The safety crown is the only hope for people in the king business
—Courtesy Minneapolis Journal.

2.8: "The King Business"
Source: *The Representative* (Minneapolis and St. Paul, MN), August 9, 1900.

This cartoon by Charles L. Bartholomew (Bart) originally appeared in the Republican Party–oriented *Minneapolis Journal*. Populist Ignatius Donnelly reprinted it in his newspaper, *The Representative*. Populist editors were not above appropriating cartoons from the mainstream press that made Populistic points. Bartholomew was referring to the rash of anarchist plots to assassinate various European monarchs. Populists claimed that monarchist excesses produced the desperate acts of anarchists. Although Populists did not condone anarchist methods, they did relish the idea of the possible demise of monarchy throughout the civilized world.

2.9: "What God Freely Gives To Man, Monopoly Appropriates"
Source: *Anthony Weekly Bulletin* (KS), April 24, 1895.

In this cartoon, God has sanctified labor by granting man the tools he needs to flourish. The landlord, however, illegitimately appropriates the proceeds. Populists argued that all value came from the physical labor involved in creating a product; this is called the labor theory of value. According to this theory, wages, rents, and interest were thinly disguised robbery by owners, landlords, and financial speculators. Today the idea sounds Marxist; in fact, Karl Marx took the idea from Adam Smith, the great proponent of laissez-faire capitalism. Populists, however, more likely got the idea from the Founding Fathers, who also read Smith's *Wealth of Nations* (1776). The idea filtered down to Populists through the ideas of Jefferson, Jackson, and Lincoln, whom Populists considered America's greatest democratic heroes.

A QUESTION FOR THE FARMERS TO CONSIDER. Copyrighted 1896.

2.10: "A Question for the Farmers to Consider"
Source: *Sound Money* (Massillon, OH), July 10, 1896.

In this cartoon by Watson Heston, John Bull, Shylock, and the mainstream political parties unfairly exploit farmers by fattening their hogs (representing banking instruments like mortgages) on the farmers' grain without reimbursing them for their labor. Such exploiters are associated with Wall Street and Britain in the background. This is another reference to the labor theory of value. According to Populists, the financial interests represented by John Bull and Shylock dominated the Democratic and Republican parties, and their wealth came from manipulating the political system.

The PEOPLE to PLUTOCRACY — Better not pile on too much, or we'll try the weight of this thing

LABOR VS. GREED. A WARNING TO PLUTOCRACY. Copyrighted 1896. by H. VINCENT.

2.11 (above): "Labor vs. Greed, A Warning to Plutocracy"
Source: *Sound Money* (Massillon, OH), July 16, 1896.

In this cartoon, the fruits of the farmers' labor are being stolen by Shylock through foreclosures, interest, rents, etc. Shylock was an easily identifiable symbol for a broad complex of greedy financial interests. The word "plutocracy" was a synonym for monopolist in the late nineteenth century. In Greek mythology, Pluto was the god of the underworld, also known as Hades. Notice that the balance bar at the top of the scales is labeled "Corrupt Legislation." Populists contended that it was corrupt legislation that allowed exploiters to steal from producers. The sword in the farmer's hand is labeled "last resort." Although farmers expressed considerable anger toward banks and mortgage companies, very little actual violence occurred.

2.12 (right): "A Modern Version of the Ancient Classics"
Source: *Republic County Freeman* (Belleville, KS), March 31, 1892.

In Greek mythology, Athena, the goddess of war, sent snakes to kill the Trojan priest Lacoön and his sons because they were about to reveal the secret of the Trojan horse. By labeling Lacoön "Labor" and the snakes "Combines," "Watered stock," "National bank system," "Trusts," "Contraction," and "Usury," cartoonist Roger Cunningham argued that greed and capitalist exploitation actually hindered honest production. Populists opposed the dominant idea that capitalist exploitation was good for the economy. Populist cartoonists produced a number of illustrations that alluded to ancient mythology, which suggest their target audience had at least some knowledge of the classics.

A WALL STREET VIEW   -New York Journal

2.13: "A Wall Street View"
Source: *Rocky Mountain News* (Denver, CO), August 24, 1896.

Ignatius Donnelly borrowed this cartoon from William Randolph Hearst's *New York Journal* for *The Representative*. The speculator on the left is an obvious glutton who has fattened himself on the labor of the farmer. Notice the skull labeled "Labor" hanging from his "Patriot" sign. Despite the speculator's responsibility for creating poverty, he is considered the patriot and the farmer an anarchist. The honest, hardworking farmer does not seem threatening, but he is considering the irony of the producer being considered the bad guy. Populist sources constantly complained of the northeastern establishment's unfair portrayal of farmers as ignorant and dangerous hicks. According to Populists, those who toiled with their hands were legitimate wealth builders, while exploiters subverted an otherwise fair distributive system. The result was a widening gap between rich and poor that encouraged victims to seek redress through radical solutions. The cartoon also suggests the speculator's actions have had a role in radicalizing the farmer.

There is nothing left for the old man but the stalks and the Republican party.

2.14: "Our Farmers' Situation"
Source: *The Representative* (Minneapolis and St. Paul, MN), October 21, 1896.

The backbreaking toil of the farmer represented in this cartoon is very poorly rewarded, but he still clings to the Republican Party as if it continued to represent him and his interests. However, the GOP obviously will not help him challenge the illegitimate exploiters as they take their profits. Farmers had to run the gauntlet of middlemen and landlords to make a living. Railroads, which farmers needed to get their produce to market, engaged in a number of unfair practices that hurt farmers more than other Americans. Money was scarce in the frontier West and war-torn South; this drove interest rates on farm mortgages and equipment up. By 1890, farm foreclosures were endemic. In addition, taxes rested more heavily on the farmer than any other class. America did not have an income tax between 1865 and 1913. The Supreme Court ruled an 1894 income tax law unconstitutional before it could be collected.

THERE IS MIGHTY LITTLE LEFT.

The origin of wealth is in the soil. It is enhanced by labor. The producer gives up plenty and gets back a pittance. The consumer pays dearly and receives a dole. Middlemen stand between and levy tribute.—Ram's Horn.

2.15: "There is Mighty Little Left"

Source: *Alva Review* (Oklahoma Territory), August 30, 1894.

This illustration by Frank Branch originally appeared in the *Ram's Horn,* an interdenominational social gospel magazine published in Chicago. The illustration makes the Populist point about middlemen standing between the producers and consumers in order to levy tribute. Farmers particularly complained about middlemen profits. Notice the size of the produce the farmer hands off to the banker and what he eventually gets back in return from the note shaver. The consumer's fate is about the same. According to the labor theory of value, middlemen were illegitimate exploiters rather than producers.

2.16: "If Christ Came to Washington"
Source: *Kansas Populist* (Cherryvale), June 14, 1895.

Religious concerns almost certainly played a part in Populists' moralistic orientation. In this illustration, Christ, who overturned the money changers' tables in the house of the Lord, evicts financial interests from Congress. The identification tags on the interlopers include a litany of villainous activities that Populists found reprehensible—bribes, land grants, and subsidies. This cartoon was inspired by publication of *If Christ Came to Congress* (1895), an early exposé of Washington corruption by Populist congressman Milford Howard of Alabama.

While the G. O. P. Slept, the A. P. A. Gathered About It and Bound It Securely
to the Earth.   And There It Is!—*After Gulliver.*

2.17: "While the GOP Slept, the APA Gathered About It and Bound It Securely to The
Earth. And There It Is!"
Source: *Rocky Mountain News* (Denver, CO), September 19, 1894.

The American Protective Association was the most important anti-Catholic organization in America during the 1890s. Although many viewed the People's Party as
an evangelical Protestant movement, people representing a wide variety of denominations (including Catholics) could be found in third-party ranks. In Texas, for instance,
Polish Catholic farmers voted overwhelmingly Populist in 1896, and a Populist organized the first Catholic services in the Oklahoma Territory. In the mid-1890s, the Populist *Rocky Mountain News* mounted a prominent campaign against the APA, which
received most of its support from Republican Party loyalists. In this illustration, APA
members are shown with caps reminiscent of the Ku Klux Klan in order to associate
them with undemocratic terrorist tactics.

2.18: "The Powers That Be"
Source: *American Nonconformist* (Winfield, KS), April 12, 1888, September 18, 1890, and July 14, 1892.

Populists feared that concentration of wealth would destroy the economic independence that Americans needed to be political free agents. European-style monarchy constituted the major threat to America's democratic institutions during the nineteenth century. Populist cartoonists particularly enjoyed throwing the enemy's most indiscreet statements back in their face. Third-party activists argued that the result of the widening gap between rich and poor would eventually destroy all of the common people's liberties. "The powers that be" would become so powerful that they would permanently establish their positions of privilege and become a traditional aristocracy in the European fashion. Notice soldiers are necessary to force the toilers to carry the sedan chair in which the plutocrats ride. Soldiers, militia, or private corporate-hired armies decided a number of labor disputes during the 1880s and 1890s. Populists considered this to be a betrayal of the long-standing Anglo-American tradition against standing (large peacetime) armies. Ironically, Americans inherited this tradition from Britain. Notice that because the toiling masses on the left and right are forced to pull the carriage in opposite directions, the coach is going nowhere. This is a negative commentary on robber baron assertions that it was their leadership that produced national progress.

TWILIGHT AMUSEMENT IN OKLAHOMA.

2.19: "Twilight Amusement in Oklahoma"
Source: *American Nonconformist* (Winfield, KS), May 2, 1889.

In a series of land runs beginning in 1889, the federal government opened the Oklahoma Territory (the western half of the present-day state of Oklahoma) to white settlement. This territory contained the last really sizeable plot of farmable land in the United States. Thus, many considered it to be their last chance to obtain the American dream of economic independence in farming. In keeping with the ambience of the times, the federal government employed the most Darwinistic method possible to make the land available, the land run. Because opening Oklahoma to settlement essentially ended the frontier, many pondered its meaning. Free land went to the fastest or, in many cases, the biggest bully. For Populists, the land runs signified social Darwinism run rampant, an extremely exploitative future for the nation. This cartoon appeared in the *American Nonconformist* of Winfield, Kansas, one of the jumping-off points for the land runs, two weeks after the first Oklahoma land run in 1889.

THE MONOPOLISTIC MILL.

2.20: "The Monopolistic Mill"
Source: *Sound Money* (Massillon, OH), June 16, 1896.

In this cartoon by Watson Heston, Presidents Grover Cleveland (Democrat, 1885–89 and 1893–97) and Benjamin Harrison (Republican, 1889–93) do the bidding of plutocracy in grinding up labor to enhance corporate profits. Notice Columbia and Uncle Sam are sharing the fate of labor, and Plutocracy, in the form of Shylock, takes the proceeds. The illustration suggests that major party leaders worked in the interest of plutocratic greed.

"MY PRICE, OR GO WITHOUT."

2.21: "My Price, or Go Without"
Source: *Morgan's Buzz Saw* (Hardy, AR), June 1, 1896.

   Antimonopoly was the theme that held all Populists together. W. Scott Morgan, editor of Morgan's *Buzz Saw,* was also editor of the National Reform Press Association's ready-print syndication. He occasionally reprinted cartoons from non-Populist newspapers like the *New York Herald,* which shared third party's antimonopoly orientation. In this illustration, a grossly bloated monopoly uses his position to overcharge labor for the things that make his life bearable—ice, sugar, tobacco, coal, and oil.

MONOPOLY WINS.

2.22: "Monopoly Wins"
Source: *Rocky Mountain News* (Denver, CO), November 22, 1892.

According to Populists, monopoly was the source of poverty and oppression, especially in the wake of the 1892 Homestead strike (in Pittsburgh). The strike actually was a lockout by Carnegie Steel Company designed to break the Amalgamated Association of Iron and Steel workers, with which Carnegie had a contract. Violence occurred when strikebreakers and Pinkertons (detectives that formed a private army for many corporations during the late nineteenth century) tried to intervene. They were unsuccessful because many townspeople sided with the strikers. Eventually, the state militia put down the strike. Populism in Colorado, where the cartoon appeared, primarily was a labor movement of silver miners; thus, there was a great deal of interest in the fate of fellow industrial workers back east.

TAKING THE LAST SHIRT OFF THE BACK OF THE LABORING MAN.

2.23: "Taking the Last Shirt..."
Source: *Southern Mercury* (Dallas, TX), July 9, 1896.

A well-heeled tax collector takes the last possessions of the poor out-of-work laborer in this cartoon from Texas, where laborers generally sided with the Populist Party. Again, government policy is seen as harming the honest producer and his family. Taxes favored the rich during the Gilded Age. When the tariff was not prohibitive, it was a consumer tax that disproportionately hurt the poor. The other great source of taxes was the land. Corporate interests appeared to avoid taxation altogether. Populists called for a graduated income tax that would make the rich share the tax burden.

"THOU ART THE MAN."

2.24: "Thou Art the Man"
Source: *Anthony Weekly Bulletin* (KS), September 13, 1895.

Columbia (a symbol of the nation) lays the blame for destitution on usurious interest rates. As exponents of the labor theory of value, Populists considered those who loaned money at interest (as a business) to be illegitimate exploiters. The original meaning of usury was loaning money at any interest; the modern definition is loaning money at exorbitant interest. Interest rates generally were higher in the developing West and South than the industrialized Northeast and Midwest. Industry was more lucrative than farming during the Gilded Age.

THE PEOPLE'S CELEBRATION.

2.25: "The People's Celebration"
Source: *Rocky Mountain News* (Denver, CO), February 19, 1896.

By 1896, America was several years into its worst depression up to that time. Business closings caused massive unemployment and many laborers lost their homes through foreclosure. For many, the economic miracle that business spokesmen claimed their leadership had brought to America appeared to vanish. Thus, the sarcastic title of this cartoon, "The People's Celebration," proved to be rather poignant.

A SOUTH AMERICAN
HALF BREED WHEAT
FARMER LIVES ON 18 CENTS
A DAY.

AN INDIAN WHEAT
FARMER LIVES ON
3 CENTS A DAY.

AN EGYPTIAN COTTON
GROWER LIVES ON
12 CENTS A DAY

A NOTE-OF WARNING.

2.26: "A Note of Warning"
Source: *Alliance Gazette* (Hutchinson, KS), June 5, 1894.

   There was a widening gap between rich and poor in Gilded Age America. This cartoon warns American farmers that they could share the fate of destitute non-European producers if contemporary trends continued. Populists feared that the downward economic mobility of the American labor force would degrade the republic to the equivalent of an oppressed colony of Europe. American republicanism required widespread property ownership, which would give the individual the economic independence needed to defend his liberties.

Chapter 3

The Campaign of Education

THE EGALITARIAN THIRD PARTIES OF THE GILDED AGE grew out of some of the era's nominally nonpartisan producer groups. The Greenback and Greenback-Labor parties drew heavily from the Patrons of Husbandry, or Grange, for their rank and file support. The Knights of Labor provided a similar service for the Union Labor Party. The Farmers' Alliances, and particularly the more aggressive Southern Farmers' Alliance, would provide much of the early support for the People's Party.

The Southern Farmers' Alliance had been founded in central Texas in 1877. It struggled along without much consequence until 1884 when S. O. Daws became a traveling lecturer. Armed with a cooperative message and the power to appoint organizers and establish suballiances, Daws and his subordinates spread the Alliance throughout Texas over the next two years. In their wake came trade agreements with local merchants, cooperative stores where merchants proved intransigent, and Alliance yards for the bulk sale of cotton. The Alliance appealed mostly to small landowners; middlemen, creditors, and the business community proved hostile. The Alliance's message educated farmers as to their interests as an oppressed economic group. Thus, collective action resulted in a growing class consciousness among farmers and rural laborers.[1]

Pivotal to farmer radicalism was the belief that nonproducers had rigged the economic system through their control of politics in order to amass wealth into their own hands. The National Banking Acts of the Civil War period had placed monetary policy in the hands of northeastern bankers. Railroad land grants had squandered millions of acres on corporations. Mortgage companies foreclosed on tens of thousands of farms between 1888 and 1892. And foreign

---

[1] McMath, *American Populism,* chaps. 2 and 3.

44

investors bought up the public domain seemingly for speculative purposes. Only the mobilization of independent producers could counter this threat to America's egalitarian traditions. Farmers had organized the Farmers' Alliances to divert America from this path. Although Alliance economic efforts were successful for a while, most eventually went bankrupt. Many Alliancemen were ready for political action when they met in convention in Cleburne, Texas, in August 1886. The meeting produced a list of demands calling for the incorporation of unions and cooperative stores, fair taxation of railroads, railroad regulation, outlawing of trade in agricultural futures, greenbacks,[2] and several pro-labor items. Conservative Alliancemen could not abide such government intervention and immediately formed a rival Alliance. Alliance president Charles W. Macune eventually averted a fratricidal war with a proposal to establish a state Alliance Exchange. He claimed that centralizing cooperative efforts would improve the Alliance's buying and selling power. The Texas Alliance Exchange would handle cotton, implements, dry goods, groceries, and general supplies at a savings to farmers in middlemen fees. Unfortunately, it was severely undercapitalized and extended credit too freely. Bankruptcy came in the summer of 1889. Similar exchanges in other states also eventually failed. Alliance leaders publicly ascribed the failures to banker and merchant hostility.[3]

The Alliance committed itself to organizing the rest of the South at Cleburne. Lecturers from Texas blanketed Dixie in 1886, leaving thousands of suballiances in their wake. Their success can be attributed to the policy of sending organizers to areas of their former residence. This gained them easy access into already existing social networks. When the producers of jute bagging (which farmers used to bale cotton) raised prices 60 percent in 1888, the Alliance was strong enough to sponsor a successful boycott. Texan Richard M. Humphries, who had been active in the Union Labor Party, led a separate Colored Farmers' Alliance, which also spread throughout the South at this time.[4]

As Alliance lecturers spread the cooperative message, they taught the concept of an irrepressible conflict between producers and exploiters. Farmers were asked to reject the robber barons' view that contemporary trends signified progress for the nation. Instead, they should rationally examine how producers' influence over the course of national development had declined. Farmers should no longer blindly accept the elite's explanation of political economy. The essence of Populism would be the profound belief that politicians had lost touch with voters

---

[2] Greenbacks were paper money not backed by gold or silver that were issued by government fiat during the Civil War. The federal government reclaimed the last greenbacks of the nineteenth century with gold in 1879.

[3] Goodwyn, *Populist Moment,* 42–58; and Tindall, "The People's Party," 1710–11.

[4] McMath, *American Populism,* 95–96.

and must be replaced by authentic representatives of the people. To them, that was the true meaning of democracy.[5]

Before citizens could take the political system away from the robber barons, they first had to be educated in the workings of the economic and political system. This meant providing an educational alternative to the public schools, the mainstream parties, and the big city presses, which Populists considered the sources of capitalist miseducation. Only with information from producer sources could they critically examine the workings of the economic and political systems and counter the robber barons' contention that contemporary trends were inevitable and progressive. Then producers could reestablish democratic control over the nation and its resources.

The debate over the loss of equality inevitably led to discussion of women's rights. Historian Charles Postel has recently noted that the Farmers' Alliance, by opening its ranks to women, provided a forum for the debate of the "woman question." Rural life often lacked the physical separation of home and work that underpinned the elite-sanctioned doctrine of "separate spheres," which assigned women to exclusively domestic roles. Commitment to women's voting rights was particularly strong in the West. Colorado and Idaho adopted women's suffrage under Populist auspices, but the culturally more conservative South resisted. Southern Populists probably were more advanced on the issue than Democrats, but they were not willing to cloud the economic issues by advocating controversial noneconomic demands. Thus, Populists' national and southern state platforms failed to include women's rights issues.[6]

Intimately connected to the women's rights issue, and also studiously avoided by most party platforms, was the liquor issue. Some Populists opposed putting restrictions on liquor out of a commitment to personal liberty, but most probably did not. Consumption of alcohol was popularly associated with squandering the family's badly needed resources, as well as with wife and child abuse. In addition, liquor interests regularly financed a wide variety of antireform efforts. In large cities, political bosses held party meetings in saloons specifically to discourage participation by women. The only women to be found in most nineteenth-century taverns were "ladies of the evening."[7]

In 1889, the Southern, Northern, and Colored Farmers' Alliances met with the Farmers' Mutual Benefit Association and Knights of Labor in St. Louis with an eye toward unification. The race issue and secret ritual of the Southern Alliance eventually caused the Northern Alliance to decline formal affiliation. Still,

---

[5] Mitchell, *Political Education*, 57, 95.

[6] Postel, *Populist Vision*, 69–102. Other good sources on Populism and women are Goldberg, "*An Army of Women*"; and Barthelme, *Women in the Texas Populist Movement*.

[7] Lebsock, "Women and American Politics," 38–41.

the platforms produced by both orders were stridently antimonopoly. The Kansas and Dakota delegations of the Northern Alliance subsequently defected to the more radical Southern Alliance, which immediately began organizing the Plains and West.[8]

At the St. Louis conference, Charles Macune unveiled a plan to solve the problem of underfinanced cooperatives. He called for the federal government to establish warehouses (called subtreasuries) to store farmers' crops. Instead of dumping their crops on the market at harvest time when it was glutted, farmers could store their crops in a subtreasury and use them as collateral for government loans of up to 80 percent of the market value of their crop. The resulting warehouse receipts could be used to pay debts. This would expand the money supply at harvest time when more money was needed, and contract it as receipt holders sold their crops. The subtreasury plan rapidly became something of an article of faith with Alliancemen.[9]

When the Southern and Colored Alliances met in Ocala, Florida, in December 1890, westerners advocated immediate third-party action. Although the Alliance was formally nonpartisan, many of its demands could be realized only through political action. Republican leaders in the Plains states had responded in an antagonistic and demeaning fashion. Southerners, however, wanted to give reform within the Democratic Party a chance. Alliance president Leonidas L. Polk of North Carolina declared "education" to be the Alliance's most immediate requirement. To effectively break voter allegiance from the mainstream parties required more evangelizing and the establishment of sources of information independent of mainstream influences. As Robert C. McMath has noted, the textbook trust presented "a politically correct version of history and economics...that celebrated the rise of industrial capitalism." Alliancemen would have to overcome this dogma in the classrooms of the suballiances before a third party could be successful. They also needed an alternative source of education and news. Thus, the Ocala meeting founded the National Reform Press Association (NRPA), which quickly became the Alliance and Populist Party's independent news service. It dispensed ready-print literature on economics, history, and politics, along with original cartoons and classroom lessons, to hundreds of newspapers nationwide. Macune successfully proposed that the decision on forming a third party be put off until the presidential election year of 1892.[10]

---

[8] Goodwyn, *Populist Moment,* 108–13.

[9] Historian Lawrence Goodwyn has contended that the cooperative-subtreasury efforts of the Alliance created a distinctive culture of protest that led to Populism, but farmer dissidence had been grounded in the protest culture of republicanism long before the 1880s; *Democratic Promise,* 313–16.

[10] McMath, *American Populism,* 148–50.

By the National Reform Press Association

THE NEW STATUE OF LIBERTY ENLIGHTENING THE PEOPLE.

3.1: "The New Statue of Liberty Enlightening the People"
Source: *Anthony Weekly Bulletin* (KS), December 14, 1894.

As a true third party and not a splinter group only dividing one of the old parties, the Populist Party needed to draw supporters from both the Democratic and Republican Parties. They did so by claiming Democratic and Republican party politicians had betrayed their Jeffersonian and Lincolnian heritages by supporting monopoly and corporate interests. In fact, many Populists claimed that they did not leave their old parties so much as their old parties left them by selling out to corporate interests. In this illustration, the new Statue of Liberty, labeled "People's Party," would enlighten voters about old-party betrayal with the "Truth."

THE TRUE SOLUTION.

A COMMON CITIZENSHIP-COMMON INTERESTS.

HOOPPOLE TOWNSHIP, POSEY COUNTY INDIANA, PEOPLE'S PARTY CLUB.

The members of this club, in their several industrial organizations, are strictly non-partisan students of political economy. As free and sovereign American citzens and voters they are enthusiastic and loyal people's party men.
George Ward

3.2: "The True Solution"
Source: *Republic County Freeman* (Belleville, KS), February 4, 1892.

Populists looked to a unity of interests among producers as the backbone of their party. A number of farmer and labor organizations educated their membership as to the cause of their distress and possible solutions in nominally nonpartisan producer organizations before moving to political action. The organizations represented in this illustration are (left to right) the Southern Farmers' Alliance, Farmers' Mutual Benefit Association, Northern Farmers' Alliance, Patrons of Industry, American Federation of Labor, Knights of Labor, Brotherhood of Locomotive Engineers, Citizens' Alliance, and Colored Farmers' Alliance (which had a white president).

THE SAME OLD GAG; NOW THEY CALL IT

"Reciprocity" or "Tariff for Revenue!"

3.3: "'Reciprocity' or 'Tariff for Revenue!'"
Source: *American Nonconformist* (Winfield, KS), April 30, 1891.

Populists contended that mainstream politicians promoted partisan conflict as a diversion so they could rob their own supporters. Notice the politicians' right hands are in the pockets of their own supporters. The words "Extortion" and "Robbery" in the bottom left-hand corner of this illustration suggest that the old parties really differed very little on the issues. Populists wished to redirect political discourse from the issues that mainstream party politicians found rewarding to issues that they believed more clearly addressed the people's interests. Education would be necessary to get voters to see the truth. This cartoon appeared at least six times in the *American Nonconformist* (with varying titles) between May 10, 1888, and October 22, 1892. It also appeared in the *Payne County Populist* (Stillwater, Oklahoma Territory) on September 7, 1894.

Bark up lively, my hungry pups! The one that strikes the key note, and keeps it up, shall have the prize.

3.4: "Bark up Lively, my Hungry Pups…"
Source: *Southern Mercury* (Dallas, TX), May 21, 1896.

Although mainstream politicians misled the people, they in turn were controlled by special interests (particularly financial interests), Populists claimed. Financiers, bankers, the gold standard, and the "money power" were the root cause of the people's distress. The labor theory of value made their professions illegitimate. In this cartoon, the Wall Street representative of the gold syndicate (Shylock) demonstrates the economic elite's control over the mainstream politicians, who appear eager to do Wall Street's bidding in return for political preferment. The politicians identified are prominent Democrats and Republicans. Explaining the connections between financial interests (the money power) and politics was an integral part of educating producers.

HI, LA, UP WE GO. SAY, GROVER, YOU HOLLER FREE TRADE AND I'LL SING RECIPROCITY   "TARIFF IS THE ISSUE FOR '92

3.5: "Hi La, Up We Go…"
Source: *American Nonconformist* (Winfield, KS), October 10, 1890.

   As with all third-party efforts in American history, Populists found it necessary to distinguish themselves from their mainstream rivals. The most effective method of doing this was to assert that they provided a real alternative that the mainstream parties did not. Notice the Tweedledee and Tweedledum on the teeter-totter's crossbar. On the left sits the Democratic candidate, Grover Cleveland, and on the right sits Republican Benjamin Harrison, the incumbent president. Both Democrats and Republicans preferred to campaign on the tariff issue in 1892. According to this illustration, they did so on the backs of their constituents.

OUR POLITICAL INFERNO. "Here the brute Harpies make their nests. • • • Men once were we, That now are rooted here !"—DANTE'S INFERNO, Canto XIII.

3.6: "Our Political Inferno"
Source: *Sound Money* (Massillon, OH), June 12, 1896.

Major party politicians are portrayed as trees rooted in Dante's *Inferno* for their sins against the people. Notice the major party's issues of protection, monometalism, and free trade are portrayed as Shylock's nests and that his trusts are nesting in both the free trade and protection nests. In this way, the artist, Watson Heston, declares the tariff a false issue. At the bottom, Shylock, again as a vulture, has devoured prosperity. This cartoon assumed a significant knowledge of literature in the prospective reader, which belies opponents' portrayal of Populists as ignorant hicks.

HOW TO LIFT THAT MORTGAGE.

3.7: "How to Lift That Mortgage"
Source: *Kansas Populist* (Cherryvale), October 18, 1895.

This cartoon portrays voting the Populist ticket as the most effective method of avoiding foreclosures. Populists expressed great confidence in the ultimate fairness of the democratic process and advocated political solutions as opposed to direct actions like labor strikes and violence. In this cartoon, Watson Heston portrays the mortgage as an octopus threateningly hanging over the home with President Grover Cleveland and Secretary of the Treasury John Carlisle, along with Republican former Secretary of the Treasury John Sherman and Shylock desperately attempting to lower the mortgage on the home. Notice that Sherman is portrayed as the devil, with a long tail and horns. Populists thought it necessary to villainize such prominent mainstream party spokesmen to wean voters from their former political affiliations.

How the Voting Cattle Obey the Will of the "Powers that Be."--(*Will show the "Powers That Be" in our Next*

3.8: "How the Voting Cattle Obey the Will of the 'Powers That Be'"
Source: *American Nonconformist* (Winfield, KS), March 22, 1888.

In this cartoon drawn for the proto-Populist Union Labor Party in 1888, Watson Heston derides voters for allowing old party bosses to lead them to the polls like cattle. Notice that almost every word on the sign reading "wimmen air tew ignerunt tew vote" is misspelled. Such ignorance could be cured only through the campaign for education. Although Populists designated economic issues as paramount, most appeared to support women's suffrage, at least outside the South. Even in the South, Populists were more favorable toward women's issues than their Democratic Party counterparts.

ASSASSINATION! The Last Resort of the Plutocracy.

THE CAMPAIGN OF EDUCATION!

Political Ignorance is the Politician's Pride   The above is the kind of work which "Carried Kansas" and is the only hope of the Nation

3.9 (left): "Assassination! The Last Resort of the Plutocracy"
Source: *American Nonconformist* (Winfield, KS), July 30, 1891.

Watson Heston portrays Plutocracy's actions as illegitimate in this illustration, which is a commentary upon the private detectives and armies hired by corporate interests to quell labor disputes. The smoke cloud labeled "Coffeyville" on the left side refers to an 1886 Kansas bomb blast that Republicans blamed on Henry and Leo Vincent, the proprietors of the *American Nonconformist*. The *Nonconformist* editors in turn claimed it was a Republican plot to discredit the Union Labor Party in the wake of Chicago's Haymarket bombing earlier that same year. In Chicago, eight avowed anarchists were convicted in a highly publicized, and rather unfair, trial for the Haymarket bombing. An 1893 Kansas legislative investigation of the Coffeyville bombing was inconclusive, but sympathetic toward the *Nonconformist* editors. The Vincents had moved to Indianapolis in 1891.

3.10 (above): "The Campaign of Education"
Source: *American Nonconformist* (Winfield, KS), July 9, 1891.

Populist authors produced a large number of book-length treatises during the late nineteenth century. Authors who affiliated with the People's Party included Edward Bellamy (*Looking Backward*), Ignatius Donnelly (*Caesar's Column*), and Terence Powderly (Grand Master Workman, or president, of the Knights of Labor). Populists also read books with a Populistic bent by non-Populists, such as Henry George's *Progress and Poverty*. Central to the Populist appeal was the belief that once people had been educated on the causes of their plight, they would join the People's Party. The book and newspaper titles listed in this illustration accurately refer to real publications. This cartoon also appeared (with varying titles) in the *American Nonconformist* twice in 1892 and a redrawn version appeared in the *Oklahoma Representative* (Guthrie) on July 2, 1896.

3.11: "Stay Out/Come In"
Source: *Ottawa Journal and Triumph* (KS), June 28, 1894; and *Rockdale Messenger* (TX), August 9, 1894.

By opening its ranks to women, the proto-Populist Southern Farmers' Alliance provided a forum for debating women's rights. Western Populists generally supported women's suffrage. Southern Populists, who worked in a more conservative environment, were more favorable toward women's issues than Democrats, but feared promoting women's rights would distract from economic issues; thus, they usually did not pursue women's issues with much vigor. This illustration, which appeared in both Kansas and Texas, portrayed the Republican Party as being cynical in its commitment to women's issues. The cartoon originated in Kansas, where the Republican Party dominated. Notice the jug of liquor next to the Republican Party door. The GOP also liked to portray itself as the party of prohibition in Kansas.

"REPRESENT ME AS TRAMPING ON A SERPENT."

3.12: "Represent Me as Tramping on a Serpent"
Source: *Kansas City Star* (MO), January 2, 1894.

    Mary Elizabeth Lease of Kansas was the most notable female spokeswoman for the Alliance and Populist Party in the 1890s. Her advice for farmers "to raise less corn and more Hell," which is possibly apocryphal, was the most quoted phrase of the Populist Revolt. The anti-Populist press loved to portray Ms. Lease as threateningly masculine. Lease was quite tall for a woman of her day and spoke with a very strong voice. Her activities questioned mainstream society's assigned gender roles, which saw women's place being in the home as opposed to the speaker's stump. Notice the gentlemen in this illustration are a bit taken aback by Lease's strident gesture and words.

INDEPENDENCE DAY—COLORADO.

3.13: "'Independence Day'—Colorado"
Source: *Rocky Mountain News* (Denver, CO), July 4, 1894.

Most western Populists supported women's suffrage. Colorado adopted women's suffrage under Populist auspices. By publishing this cartoon on Independence Day, the *Rocky Mountain News* associated women's issues with the egalitarian promise of the republicanism of the American Revolution. Having both a man and a woman celebrating suggested women's suffrage was a victory for both. Populist Governor Davis H. Waite, who strongly promoted the issue, was later disappointed that most of the newly enfranchised voters did not flock to the People's Party. Instead, they cast their ballots exactly the same as their husbands.

3.14: "Little Red School House"
Source: *Southern Mercury* (Dallas, TX), November 26, 1891.

In this illustration, the Grange, Farmers' Mutual Benefit Association (FMBA), and Farmers' Alliance join the Woman's Christian Temperance Union (WCTU) in evicting the bartender and his patrons (which include the devil) from a saloon and turning it into the "Little Red School House." Populists generally supported such issues as pro-family. Although the People's Party preferred to emphasize economic issues, there was a community of interests among farm organizations and other reformers. In the 1890s, prohibition was considered a liberal, women's issue. Drinking was associated in the popular mind with wife and child abuse, destitution, and broken homes. The WCTU was broadly reformist and formally endorsed much of the Alliance/Populist program.

3.15: "Whiskey Trust"
Source: *American Nonconformist* (Indianapolis, IN), May 5, 1892.

 Liquor interests financed conservative political causes in order to stave off regulation during the nineteenth and early twentieth centuries. Notice that the barrel dispensed money to both Democrats and Republicans. Columbia in the form of the People's Party is about to break the corrupt link between the old parties and liquor interests with a sword labeled "Temperance." By portraying liquor interests as a trust, this cartoon plays upon the Populist's antimonopoly theme, which made liquor doubly threatening.

THE BALLOT IS OUR WEAPON.

3.16: "The Ballot Is Our Weapon"
Source: *American Nonconformist* (Indianapolis, IN), November 3, 1892.

Populists emphasized democratic political solutions to their problems. In this allegory of David and Goliath, the people use the ballot to defeat capitalism and its subsidized press. Notice that David (the people) has social science on his side, while Goliath used ignorance and boodle (bribed) legislatures as his shield to defend capitalism. For many, the word "capitalist" (and capitalism) had a narrower meaning before the Bolshevik Revolution (1917). Essentially, it meant "investor" or "one who used capital" as opposed to one who labors for a living.

PLUTOCRACY HAS A NEW METHOD OF MAKING EVERYTHING APPEAR ALL RIGHT TO THE PEOPLE.

The gold standard press of the United States, which is chiefly printed in the larger cities, is either directly or indirectly owned and operated by British capital, While these organs of treason confined their operations to their own cities not so much fault was found. The patriotic country press would still stand for American principles. In order to break down the power of the country press the prices of the metropolitan papers were reduced from 8 to 2 and 1 cent a copy. The railroads and news companies (offsprings of same British sire) aided the invasion of the little country towns by arranging time tables so as to carry the city papers to the farthest distance on day of issue. The flood gates of this sort of pollution are now wide open and the country people are paying a penny a day for the privilege of hearing that the British gold standard is all right, that government by injunction is all right, that thievery in public office is all right, that the bribing of legislatures is all right, that decent pictures and immoral theatre plays are all right, that divorces are all right, that family scandals are all right, that treason to the Constitution is all right, that indecent advertisements are all right, in short that everything that is wrong is right. May God, in some way, protect the public conscience from this form of degeneracy.—From a Recent Speech.

3.17: "Plutocracy Has a New Way of Making Everything Appear All Right to the People"
Source: *Norman People's Voice* (Oklahoma Territory), November 5, 1897.

Although the Populist press provided an alternative news source, it must have seemed an impossible task to counter the influence of big-city daily newspapers. Well-financed big-city daily newspapers had large editorial staffs and used power-driven presses to flood the nation with anti-Populist literature; thus, the country press, which has right on its side, is swamped under by its big-city opponent. Notice that the city newspaper's editorial room is staffed by monkeys that mindlessly mimic the capitalist propaganda they are fed. Because of inflation, the $50,000 city press would be worth more than $1 million today.

PUT NONE BUT AMERICANS ON
GUARD.

3.18: "Put None But Americans on Guard"
Source: *Anthony Weekly Bulletin* (KS), June 7, 1895.

This cartoon notes the foreign connections of some of the nation's leading mainstream party editors and publishers. Joseph Pulitzer was a native of Austria-Hungary (not Germany as this cartoon suggests). James Gordon Bennett Jr. ran the *New York Herald* by telegram from Paris. E. L. Godkin was the son of a Protestant minister living in Ireland, which was part of Great Britain at the time. Charles Ransom Miller of the *New York Times* was American-born, but pro-British in his sympathies. Associating the major New York newspapers with foreign interests suggests they were tools of alien interests.

Populist—You see, Uncle Sam, that the X Rays thrown on this old party combination brings out plainly the inwardness of their actions.
Uncle Sam—Yes, it is plain to me now where the whole movement was concocted.

3.19: "The X-Rays"
Source: *Sound Money* (Massillon, OH), May 19, 1896.

In this cartoon, the Populist Party shows Uncle Sam the rottenness hidden inside the Democratic and Republican Parties. Notice the old parties are in league with Rothschild, a Jewish banking family, and John Bull. They have just emerged from hell where gold bonds (government bonds redeemable only in gold) are hatched. Such an exposé was a major function of the third party's educational program. The first medical x-ray was taken in December 1895. This cartoon, which appeared only five months later, suggests people in the American hinterland were as up-to-date as anyone else on the technological innovations of the day.

A PURELY POLITICAL, BUT STRICTLY NON-PARTISAN SCHOOL.

The alliance is a non-partisan, educational organization, and the result of its course of education is the nation's hope. The party affiliation of its individual members is purely a personal affair, voluntary and free from coercion. In the alliance the majority has no right to dictate political action to the minority, or to commit the organization to any particular party, whether it be republican, democratic or people's. But every true allianceman will act with the party that indorses its principles and vote for men who are known to be in sympathy with its objects.

3.20: "A Purely Political, But Strictly Non-Partisan School"
Source: *Republic County Freeman* (Belleville, KS), January 28, 1892.

Educating farmers in the politically neutral Southern Farmers' Alliance setting was crucial to building the People's Party. Late nineteenth-century politics was highly partisan and loyalties were strong. Political affiliation was almost akin to church membership. For this reason, the Farmers' Alliance became a valuable way station between a voter's old party and Populism. Committing farmers to issues that neither mainstream party would accept was the first step to weaning them from old party loyalties. Only when farmers realized that their old party would not support their interests was it possible to recruit them into the People's Party.

Chapter 4

Third-Party Action

I n response to GOP intransigence, third parties appeared in the Plains states in 1890. In Kansas, they swept the state House of Representatives, carried five of seven U.S. congressional seats, and named farm editor William A. Peffer to replace Republican James J. Ingalls in the U.S. Senate. The holdover Kansas Senate, however, remained Republican and sabotaged Populist efforts at reform. Third parties also won the legislature in Nebraska and elected another U.S. senator, James H. Kyle, in South Dakota. In the South, because Democrats proved decidedly more conciliatory toward the Alliance, Alliancemen attempted to work within Dixie's dominant party. In 1890, they claimed to have elected four governors, nineteen U.S. congressmen, and majorities in eight southern state legislatures.[1]

When the Southern and Colored Alliances met in Ocala, Florida, in December 1890, westerners advocated immediate third-party action. Southerners, however, wanted to give reform within the Democratic party a chance. The Ocala convention produced a platform that Populists would draw from liberally in later documents. It called for abolition of national banks, issuing greenbacks, adoption of free silver, implementation of the subtreasury plan, ending alien land ownership, instituting a graduated income tax, and government supervision of railroads. Anxious westerners called a May 1891 conference in Cincinnati, Ohio. With few southerners in attendance, however, they decided to wait to form a national party until the Alliance held its convention in St. Louis in February 1892. Although southerners also proved reticent at St. Louis, westerners went ahead with founding the People's Party and adopted a platform similar to the Ocala document. Afterward they scheduled a national nominating convention for July in Omaha. By that date, the do-nothing 1891 southern legislatures were

---

[1] Ostler, *Prairie Populism*, 9–10. The Alliance claimed to have elected governors in Georgia, South Carolina, Tennessee, and Texas. They also claimed majorities in the Alabama, Florida, Georgia, Missouri, North and South Carolina, Tennessee, and Texas legislatures.

only a bitter memory for Dixie's Alliancemen. Having given up on reform within the Democratic Party, they were ready to join the third-party movement.[2]

More than 1,300 delegates met in Omaha, Nebraska, in July 1892, to nominate a national ticket and write a platform. Leonidas L. Polk, president of the Southern Farmers' Alliance, was expected to receive the convention's highest honor. Unfortunately, he died just before the convention. Federal judge Walter Q. Gresham, who had flirted with Populist doctrines, seemed to be the next best choice, but he declined. In the end, the presidential nomination devolved upon General James B. Weaver of Iowa, the 1880 presidential candidate of the Greenback-Labor Party. As his running mate, the convention chose ex-Confederate General James G. Field of Virginia. The blue/gray ticket of Civil War veterans symbolized the party's attempt to transcend the old issues inherited from the Civil War and Reconstruction and face the problems produced by Gilded Age development.

Party leaders scheduled the presentation of the platform for the Fourth of July. It quickly became the bible of Populism. The preamble, written by novelist Ignatius Donnelly, charged that the nation was "rapidly degenerating into European conditions." "Governmental injustice," it claimed, "bred two great classes—tramps and millionaires." This degeneration was attributed to "a vast conspiracy against mankind . . . if not met and overthrown at once it forebodes terrible social convulsions, the destruction of civilization, or the establishment of an absolute despotism." The great issue, the preamble charged, was "whether we are to have a republic to administer."[3]

The Omaha Platform called for reform in land, transportation, and monetary policy. Populists demanded that public land be set aside for actual settlers rather than speculators. They called for government ownership of railroads, telephones, and telegraphs. As the platform explained, "the railroad corporations will either own the people or the people must own the railroads." Concentration of such power into the hands of a few was a threat to American liberties. On finance, Populists demanded that the northeastern-dominated National Banking System be replaced by postal savings banks directly responsible to elected officials. They also demanded a flexible currency that could be maintained at $50 per capita. This meant greenbacks (fiat money not based upon precious metals), although the platform also called for free silver. The platform likewise endorsed the subtreasury plan and contained an expression of sentiments sympathetic to labor, favoring the democratization of politics and endorsing a graduated income

[2] The Ocala, Cincinnati, and St. Louis platforms are reprinted in Hicks, *Populist Revolt,* 430–39.
[3] The Omaha Platform is reprinted in ibid., 439–44.

tax. Except for the subtreasury plan, reformers had agitated all of these issues for decades.[4]

The money issue of late nineteenth-century America quickly became the third party's premier issue. It is best viewed as a debtor-creditor rivalry. America suffered from massive deflation between 1865 and 1896. The production of goods and services expanded considerably faster than the supply of gold and silver. Americans today have lived through an extended period of inflation. Deflation, however, is much worse. Major economic depressions are characterized by deflation (consumers fail to purchase goods and services, which drives their prices down). Two of America's three worst depressions occurred during the late nineteenth century (1873–79 and 1893–97).

If a person owned a dollar in 1865, the same dollar would purchase 1.88 times as much in 1896. This means that the person owning the dollar saw its value nearly double without performing any labor. Thus, owners of wealth (the rich) benefited from deflation by obtaining considerably greater purchasing power over time. But a person who took out a loan in 1865 would have to pay the loan back with increasingly valuable dollars over time. In addition, because the per capita amount of money in circulation decreased over this period, interest rates increased. Third-party supporters blamed the metallic basis of money (gold and silver) for deflation. The production of such metals did not keep up with the production of other goods and services. Thus, Populists advocated paper money. The federal government had used greenbacks to meet expenses during the Civil War, but exchanged them for gold certificates afterward. The amount of greenbacks in circulation could be decreased or expanded in order to create monetary stability. Today, all modern industrial nations use fiat money. But most nineteenth-century Americans believed money had to have a metallic backing. Minting silver and gold at a ratio of 16 to 1 also would have reversed deflation after 1873, although to a much lesser degree than greenbacks. Advocating the "free [untaxed] coinage of silver and gold at a ratio of 16 to 1," or "free silver," however, had the advantage of avoiding the argument about the value of fiat money.

In 1873, the federal government removed silver from the U.S. mint's coinage list. The relative market values of gold and silver at the time meant that most people used gold and hoarded silver. Later in 1873, large deposits of silver ore were discovered. If the pre-1873 ratio had still been in effect, the results would have reversed deflation. In the cash-starved sections of the nation, southerners and westerners immediately labeled the new minting policy a conspiracy by the "money power." Although modern scholars have found no evidence of

[4] Ibid., 229–37, 439–44.

a conspiracy, the circumstances certainly looked suspicious to those hurt by the new policy, which became known as "the Crime of '73"[5]

Because the free-silver issue circumvented the arguments over fiat money, many inflationists (or more accurately, reflationists) found it easier to promote, and it came to overshadow the call for greenbacks. Congress periodically found it expedient to do something for silver interests to defuse their inflationist lobbying efforts. This usually meant "do something" for silver mine interests, rather than debtors. In 1878, Congress passed the Bland-Allison Act, which required the secretary of the treasury to purchase between $2 and $4 million of silver. The Treasury Department usually purchased the minimum amount at market value, but made legal tender notes redeemable only in gold, thus maintaining the gold standard. In 1890, Congress passed the Sherman Silver Purchase Act, which committed the federal government to purchasing 54 million ounces of silver a year (roughly the total American production). This was about twice the amount purchased under the Bland-Allison Act, but both of these acts avoided the bimetallic standard of 16 to 1. Thus, neither piece of legislation had a major effect upon deflation.[6] In 1892, the Democratic and Republican Parties opposed free silver in their national platforms; only the People's Party was committed to the white metal during this campaign.

Electorally, the success of the People's Party hinged upon construction of three coalitions of the dispossessed: southerners and westerners, farmers and laborers, and blacks and poor whites in the South. The rationale for these coalitions was the fact that the South and West both had colonial debtor economies, farmers and laborers shared a common status as producers, and blacks and poor white southerners frequently shared a common economic situation. The South-West coalition worked the best. Labor began to show significant interest in People's Party with the Depression of 1893. Getting poor blacks and whites to work together proved to be difficult, although there were some successes.[7]

James B. Weaver spread the Populist message with a cross-country speaking tour in 1892. He spoke before enthusiastic crowds and on election day received 1,029,846 popular votes and 22 electoral votes. It was the first time since 1860 that a third party had broken into the electoral college.

Populism was strongest in western states that had joined the Union after 1860, where the party drew mostly from farmers and miners. Other reformers supplemented their ranks in urban areas. Antimonopoly provided the unifying theme. In many western states, Democrats supported Populists to keep their states' electoral votes out of the Republican column. The People's Party elected a

[5] Clanton, *Populism,* 122; and Hicks, *Populist Revolt,* 301–4.

[6] Clanton, *Populism,* 122–23; and Hicks, *Populist Revolt,* 305–6.

[7] Woodward, *Origins of the New South,* 252.

governor and state senate in Kansas, but Republicans disputed returns that would have also given them the state House of Representatives. The newly elected Populist governor, Lorenzo D. Lewelling, a Quaker and pacifist, eventually backed down in the potentially violent "Kansas legislative war" of 1893.[8]

In the South, Populists arranged coalition tickets with Republicans in Alabama and Louisiana, but formal association with the party of Reconstruction was too much for white Populists in most southern states. Serious efforts, however, were made to wean blacks from the GOP. In Texas, third-party leaders named two African Americans to their state executive committee. Democrats consequently attempted to blunt the third-party appeal by endorsing some Populist issues in Georgia, Texas, Florida, and the Carolinas. In South Carolina, Democratic governor Ben Tillman even endorsed the subtreasury plan, which left the third party stillborn in his state. Populists did best in Alabama, where fraud probably carried the day for Democrats. Fraud also accounted for the defeat of Alliance Democrat-turned-Populist congressman Tom Watson's reelection bid in Georgia. He had made a public appeal for African American support for the People's Party in *The Arena,* a reform journal with a national readership.[9]

Only one-half of the Alliance's southern membership voted the Populist ticket in 1892. Deserting the white man's party less than a generation after Reconstruction was too high a price for many, despite the educational efforts of the Alliance. Democratic racial demagoguery, fraud, and violence also took their toll. Southern Populists did better among white voters than among African Americans. Blacks were hesitant to relinquish their power base in the GOP, and the Populist economic program spoke primarily to the interests of landowners, not tenants. Still, where white Populists provided physical protection to blacks (which was their primary concern in this era), biracial coalitions frequently proved successful.[10]

Populists fared badly in the Midwest and Northeast, where close rivalries between mainstream parties provided alternatives within the traditional two-party system. Likewise, the Populist appeal failed to attract large numbers of northeastern and midwestern laborers. Solidarity between the Alliance and the Knights of Labor in the South and West translated into farmer-labor unity partly because both generally came from the same ethnic groups. But recent immigrant laborers in the Midwest and Northeast frequently were not unionized and viewed evangelical WASP reform movements with suspicion. Fatefully, many suballiances, which had provided a politically neutral setting for educating

---

[8] For more on the 1893 Kansas legislative war, see Clanton, *Populism,* 131–36.

[9] Goodwyn, *Democratic Promise,* 290–91; Tindall, "The People's Party," 1717; and Watson, "Negro Question in the South," 540–50.

[10] Clanton, *Populism,* 96–97; Goodwyn, *Populist Moment,* 121–24; and McMath, *American Populism,* 172–73.

prospective Populists, transformed themselves into Populist clubs in 1892. This meant that they would no longer provide a seemingly nonpartisan educational way station from old party to new.[11]

---

[11] In 1902, ex-Alliancemen founded the National Farmers' Union as a conscious resurrection of the Southern Farmers' Alliance. This time they promised to keep the farm order strictly nonpartisan and to work within the mainstream parties. It still operates today as a representative of small farmer interests. See Miller, "Building a Progressive Coalition in Texas," 176–77.

THE HOGG ADMINISTRATION BEFORE THE HOUSTON CONVENTION.

4.1: "Hogg Administration Before the Houston Convention"
Source: *Southern Mercury* (Dallas, TX), November 8, 1892.

In this illustration, Governor James Stephen Hogg of Texas rejects the farmers' petition to appoint Allianceman S. D. A. Duncan to the newly established Texas Railroad Commission. Hogg hitched his star to the Southern Farmers' Alliance by supporting its demand for a regulatory railroad commission in 1890. Seeing the possibility of reform within the Democratic Party, Texas Alliancemen were hesitant to join their western brethren in a third-party effort, but Hogg made the membership of the Texas Railroad Commission appointive and declined to appoint an Allianceman to the body. N. W. "Skunk" Finley, standing behind Hogg, had kicked those committed to the Alliance's subtreasury plan out of the Democratic Party in 1891; thus, by 1892 many Alliancemen in Texas, as in other southern states, were ready for third-party action.

4.2: "The Purification of Politics Is an Iridescent Dream!!!"
Source: *American Nonconformist* (Winfield, KS), October 16, 1890.

Senator John J. Ingalls of Kansas proved to be one of the Republicans who most antagonized the Farmers' Alliance. His most infamous comment was that "the purification of politics is an iridescent dream." Populist cartoonists loved to use the enemies' own words against them. Notice that Ingalls stands on a platform of bribery, villainy, and corruption. The cloud behind Ingalls is from the Coffeyville bombing. The comment about Hessians (right center) is a reference to the British use of Hessian (German) mercenaries during the American Revolution. Farm editor William A. Peffer would replace Ingalls in the U.S. Senate in 1891.

A MIGHTY POOR EXCHANGE.
From the sublime to the ridiculous.

4.3: "A Mighty Poor Exchange"
Source: *Judge (New York City)*, April 25, 1891.

    Judge was a pro-Republican Party news magazine published in New York City. Both *Judge* and its Democratic Party rival, *Puck,* were vehemently anti-Populist. In this cartoon, which appeared in color (both *Judge* and *Puck* used color illustrations), *Judge* laments the exit of Republicans George F. Edmunds and William McKinley from the U.S. Congress in 1891, the same year Populists "Sockless" Jerry Simpson and Alfred A. "Whiskers" Peffer entered the House and Senate, respectively. The artist uses size to portray the relative merits he sees in the men. Notice both Simpson and Peffer are dressed in a rather ramshackle manner in this cartoon. Simpson, of course, wore socks. He received his nickname in a debate with a Republican Congressman whom Simpson described as follows: "This prince of the royal blood is gorgeously bedizened, his soft white hands are pretty things to look at, his feet are encased in fine silk hosiery," which contrasted significantly with his audience of poor farmers. Peffer's long beard and rustic attire quickly made him the preferred symbol of his party for opposition cartoonists who wished to portray Populists as ignorant hicks.

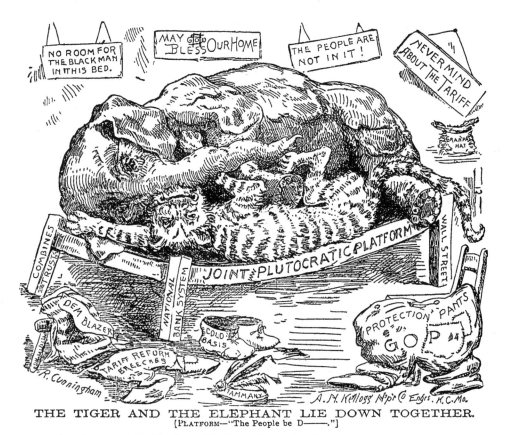

THE TIGER AND THE ELEPHANT LIE DOWN TOGETHER.
[PLATFORM—"The People be D———."]

4.4: "The Tiger and the Elephant Lie Down Together"
Source: *Alliance Gazette* (Hutchinson, KS), November 22, 1891.

In order to justify the new party's existence, Populists needed to convince voters that the Democratic and Republican parties did not offer them legitimate choices. In this cartoon, the Republican Elephant and the Democratic Party's Tammany Tiger lie somewhat uncomfortably in the same bed. Tammany Hall was the popular name for the New York City Democratic Party machine, which many viewed as particularly corrupt. The use of animals to represent human traits effectively transmitted to readers in shorthand form memorable connotations of their character—the bloated elephant and the vicious tiger. Notice the old parties lie on the "Joint Plutocracy Platform," which looks perilously close to collapsing. Populists clearly saw the major party's response to their problems as inadequate.

LET THE PEOPLE USE THE REMEDY.

The Sovereign Power Is In the Ballot Box.

4.5: "Let the People Use the Remedy"
Source: *Rocky Mountain News* (Denver, CO), February 9, 1896.

   Columbia redirects the producer's anger away from violence and toward the ballot box as a solution to the money power. Labeling financial interests the "money power" delegitimized them by association with the earlier "slave power" epithet that abolitionists used to rally sentiment against another all-powerful, conspiratorial bogeyman: the slaveholder. Although the plight of farmers and laborers was severe by the mid-1890s, Populist spokesmen constantly advised physical restraint and commitment to the democratic process. They feared the anger that injustice created would result in anarchy and discredit their cause. Labor strikes in this era frequently devolved into violence.

The conspiracy entered into by the bosses of the organized hypocrisies at the behest of the Wall street pluto-crats will fall short of its purpose, and the solid democratic south will prove to be a thing of the past As John J. In-galls has sold the west and south, if combined, are invincible. They have combined, and will send men to the halls of congress who will never vote for a force bill of any kind or nature whatsoever. Men and brethren! keep cool and close up the ranks – GEORGE C. WARD.

4.6: "The War Is Over"

Source: *Republic County Freeman* (Belleville, KS), July 28, 1892.

At the Populists' Omaha Convention of 1892, the People's Party nominated ex–Union general James B. Weaver and ex–Confederate general James G. Field for president and vice president. The blue/gray ticket symbolized Populists' attempt to overcome the Civil War and Reconstruction animosities that Democrats and Republicans employed to maintain loyalty to their parties. Republican President Benjamin Harrison (left) and Democratic presidential candidate (and former president) Grover Cleveland (right) try unsuccessfully to divert attention from the Populists. The Lodge "Force Bill" of 1890 threatened to place southern elections under federal control (in other words, to revive Reconstruction) and raised the specter of "Negro supremacy" among white southerners. Although the bill never became law, the threat it posed became a rallying point for southern Democrats, and impeded the growth of the People's Party in the South. Harrison's "Granpa" was ex-president William Henry Harrison. The fact that "Bennie's" hat seems too big suggests he had not lived up to the promise of his grandfather. General Field had lost his right leg during the Civil War. Notice the illustrator did not include his crutches in the drawing; it would have been a sign of weakness. Four decades later, President Franklin D. Roosevelt normally avoided appearing in public in his wheelchair for the same reason.

A PARTY OF PATCHES.
Grand Balloon Ascension—Cincinnati, May 20th, 1891.

4.7: "A Party of Patches"
Source: *Judge (New York City),* June 6, 1891.

This famous anti-Populist cartoon from *Judge* showed some of the most prominent and colorful Populist leaders (Terence Powderly, Ben Butler, William A. Peffer,
and "Sockless" Jerry Simpson) ascending in a balloon stitched together from patches
representing proto-Populist producer groups and previously unsuccessful third parties.
It accurately shows the groups that came together to form the People's Party, except
for anarchists and communists of course (most, but not all, socialists associated with
the Populist Party before its collapse in 1896). The artist's purpose in presenting the
party as a patchwork was to associate it with previous losing causes. Mainstream ideas
of social Darwinism supported the idea that losers had lost because they were simply
inferior. Notice the party leaders are supported by a "platform of Lunacy" and that
Peffer, who was infamous for long-winded speeches, is tossing flyers to an unseen, and
presumably nonexistent, audience.

FROM THE DENVER ROAD.

THE SINGLE GOLD STANDARD IN EUROPE

Common people of Europe want the double standard, because it more than doubles the money in circulation. When money is plentiful, as it should always be, there is no chance for anarchy, because then the people will be happy. If the nations of Europe do not return to bimetallism (double silver and gold standard), in less then 25 years there will be a vestige of monarchial power left. The present state of affairs in Europe is alarming to say the most. --New York Recorder (Republican).

4.8: "The Single Gold Standard in Europe"
Source: *Anthony Weekly Bulletin* (KS), February 9, 1894.

The preamble to the Omaha Platform was a rather apocalyptic indictment of contemporary conditions. The author, Ignatius Donnelly, charged that America was "degenerating into European conditions," a less than subtle reference to the wide gap between rich and poor in Europe, which Populists believed encouraged radicalism on the part of Europe's oppressed masses. Deflation caused by adoption of the gold standard is blamed for this circumstance. In this illustration, anarchy is presented as an angry bomb with a fuse about to go off scattering the royal heads of Europe in its wake. Americans were particularly sensitive to anarchist plots in the 1890s because of the Haymarket and Coffeyville bombings.

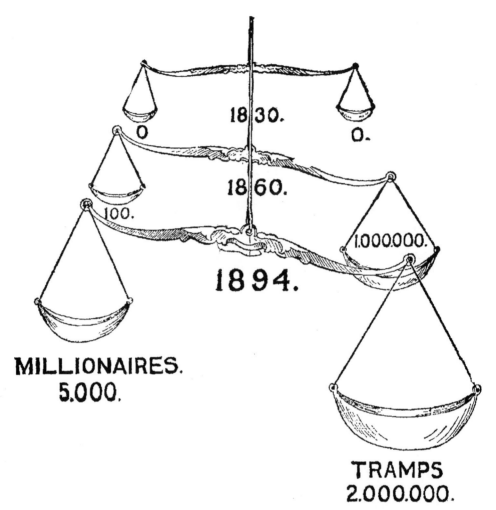

TRAMPS AND MILLIONAIRES.

Some Figures Which go to Prove that Created Millionaires Create Poverty.

4.9: "Tramps and Millionaires"
Source: *Anthony Weekly Bulletin* (KS), May 4, 1894.

The 1892 Omaha Platform also charged that "governmental injustice bred two great classes—tramps and millionaires." The widening gulf between rich and poor that appeared in late nineteenth-century America symbolized Europe's more static and unfair social system. Millionaires, they charged, obtained their wealth through illegitimate manipulation of the political system, which included protective tariffs, railroad land grants, and corporate charters. This, in turn, impoverished those who actually built the nation through their labor. In other words, the legislation that created millionaires likewise created tramps.

UNCLE SAM—"Guess I'd Better Destroy Those Suckers Growing Up from the Roots and Then the Branches Will Bear Good Fruit.'

4.10: "The People's Party Tree"
Source: *Kansas Populist* (Cherryvale), August 23, 1895.

According to Populists, the third party was necessary because the old parties had betrayed the trust of the people; thus, the People's Party had Democratic and Republican Party roots. Populists claimed to be the true inheritors of the Democratic and Republican parties' traditions as the old parties transformed themselves into tools of corporate and financial interests. Other contemporary third parties are viewed as suckers that need to be eliminated before they sap the strength of the main trunk. Populist spokesmen never tired of telling their audiences that their old parties had left them rather than vice-versa. In Texas, Alliancemen who were not willing to denounce the subtreasury plan were literally kicked out of the Democratic Party through the use of a party test.

The law condemns the men
or woman
Who steals a goose from off
the common.

But turns the greater villain
loose,
Who steals the common from
the goose

4.11: "The Law Condemns the Man or Woman..."
Source: *Payne County Populist* (Stillwater, Oklahoma Territory), January 4, 1895.

The 1892 Omaha Platform of the People's Party quickly became the bible of Populism. The land, transportation, and money planks formed a trinity of the party's most important issues. In this illustration, the land speculator is portrayed as the source of poverty and crime among those he has dispossessed.

The poem used with this illustration originated with the English enclosure movement, which drove many farmers into destitution and subservient dependence. It was centuries old by the 1890s. For Populists, and many other Americans, the enclosure movement symbolized what was wrong with the Old World. The Omaha Platform called for an end to alien land ownership. The wording was unfortunate; Democrats and Republicans misrepresented the plank as anti-immigrant. In fact, Populists wanted land set aside for actual settlers, whether immigrant or native-born, and opposed land ownership by European speculators. Foreign investment in western ranching corporations was significant by the 1890s, and this plank largely was a product of the farmer-rancher rivalry of the late nineteenth-century American West.

Signs reading "Keep Off the Grass" and "No Trespass" became common in Populist cartoons after Jacob Coxey's poor people's march on Washington in 1894. Police arrested Coxey for stepping on the White House lawn when he tried to deliver to President Cleveland a petition calling for government work projects for the unemployed. The Constitution, of course, gives citizens the right to petition their government. The event symbolized how far America had strayed from popular control of politics.

ANOTHER FEATURE OF OUR PLATFORM.

Third—Transportation being a means of exchange and a public necessity, the government should own and operate the railroads in the interest of the people.

The telegraph and telephone, like the post office system, being a necessity for the transmission of news, should be owned and operated by the government in the interest of the people.

4.12: "U.S. Railway and Telegraph Office: Another Feature of Our Platform"
Source: *Republic County Freeman* (Belleville, KS), April 14, 1892.

The second major issue the Omaha Platform addressed was transportation. Populists called for government ownership of railroads, telephones, and telegraphs. The preamble to the platform stated that "the railroad corporations will either own the people or the people must own the railroads." Populists considered the railroads, telephones, and telegraphs to be natural monopolies. This circumstance conferred upon their owners more economic (and political) power than was safe in a democratic nation. Notice that Populists expected the government to operate these natural monopolies in the interests of the people. Populists assumed government service would be more efficient than private enterprise because they would not purposefully attempt to gouge the public like privately owned enterprises. The plank was considered fairly radical, and not all Populists supported it. There was, however, always a significant socialist presence in the People's Party, which included such notables as Edward Bellamy, Eugene V. Debs, and Julius Wayland.

CAPITAL AND LABOR ON THEIR TRAVELS.

4.13: "Capital and Labor on Their Travels"
Source: *Anthony Weekly Bulletin* (KS), August 4, 1893.

Railroads were the highways of the nineteenth century. Their monopolistic practices and government subsidies raised the ire of many Americans, but especially farmers who depended on their service to get their crops to market. Railroads regularly gave free passes to politicians and other favored classes while common people had to pay for their tickets. Aside from lawmen, who might provide some protection against train robbers, the service the railroads expected from the politicians who received free passes was obviously political favoritism.

The Difference Between Working for Private Corporations and the Government.

4.14: "The Difference Between Working for Private Corporations and the Government"
Source: *Sound Money* (Massillon, OH), October 24, 1895.

Another argument Populists put forward for government ownership of the railroad was that government management would provide better wages and working conditions for railroad laborers. Private greed, which led to exploitation of labor, motivated railroad magnates. Government managers would serve the public welfare, and such fairness would result in fewer disruptive labor disputes. Notice the subservient pose of the laborer doffing his hat to a well-heeled supervisor in the upper pane. Contrast it with the proud stance of the workmen in the bottom panel.

Not a very pleasing prospect for the young man.—He gets a think on him.
REMEDY: Government ownership and control.

4.15: "Not a Very Pleasing Prospect for the Young Man"
Source: *American Nonconformist* (Indianapolis, IN), August 18, 1892.

Many laborers considered working for the railroads to be desirable because it was physically impossible to closely supervise them. But working for the railroad was one of the most dangerous jobs of late nineteenth-century America. Long hours of working around heavy machinery produced tired, less-than-cautious workers; thus, wrecks and accidents were numerous. Most railroad workers could not get life insurance at any price during the 1890s. The disheveled wreck of a man at the left, begging for sustenance, would be the end result. Presumably, government managers would balance the public's service needs with the welfare of workers better than private owners whose greed caused shortcuts that endangered workers. Railroad laborers became an important element of the Populist coalition with the Pullman strike of 1894.

RAILROAD CORPORATIONS PAY NO TAXES.

All Taxes Levied Upon Income Producing Properties, or Utilities, Are Shifted on to the Patrons and Users of Such Utilities.

"Government pays no taxes on any of its property. As it now is, the railroads pay a large proportion of the taxes for the expenses of running the state, the counties and the schools. The railroads now pay not less than $2,000,000 taxes in Kansas. If the government owned them, they would pay not a cent, but that amount of money would come out of the pockets of the farmers and other citizens of the state."—J. W. Ady, at Wichita, Kan., October 3, 1892.

Rats!!! Taxes, being one of the 'fixed charges" of railroads are included in the item "operating expenses," and are paid by the patrons of the roads. The only taxes which cannot be shifted are a poll tax; a tax upon net incomes; a tax upon land which produces no income; (such as unused vacant lands and residence sites occupied by their owners;) and a tax upon personal property kept for use and not for profit. Even under private ownership, untaxed railroads could and would reduce transportation rates by just the sum of the taxes they now pay.

4.16: "Railroad Corporations Pay No Taxes"
Source: *Republic County Freeman* (Belleville, KS), November 3, 1892.

In this illustration, producers pay fees to use the railroads into the "railroad mill," from which profits, expenses, and taxes emerge. In addition to cheating producers and wrecking laborers' lives, railroads passed the cost of taxes on to their clients. Sometimes railroads paid few or no taxes. To be part of the modern world, towns had to have railroad service, but railroads frequently blackmailed municipalities into agreements that absolved them from paying property taxes as the price of building to their towns.

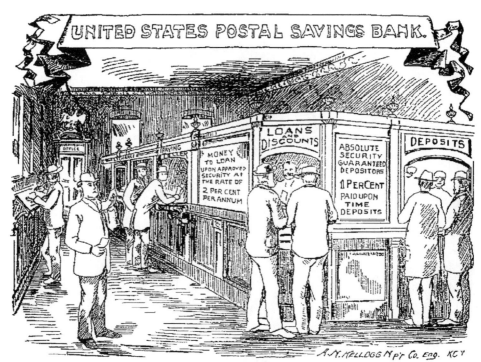

A FEATURE OF THE PLATFORM.

We demand that postal savings banks be established by the government for the safe deposit of the earnings of the people and to facilitate exchange.—St. Louis Demands, Feb. 22, 1892.

4.17: "Postal Savings Banks: A Feature of the Platform"
Source: *Republic County Freeman* (Belleville, KS), April 7, 1892.

The third, and ultimately most important, plank in the Omaha Platform involved the multifaceted money issue. Populists called for abolition of the National Banking System (which allowed bankers to control monetary policy) and establishment of government-operated postal savings banks. These proposals were designed to reclaim control of banking and currency policy from bankers and facilitate the transfer of money between the various sections of the nation. Farmers saw the efficient transfer of capital to the agricultural sections of the nation (West and South) at harvest time as essential to raising commodity prices. This flexibility was a major feature of the Federal Reserve System, which replaced the National Banking Acts in 1913. An added benefit of postal savings banks would be government responsibility for the safety of deposits, the importance of which would become obvious between 1929 and 1933 when more than five thousand American banks defaulted, wiping out the savings of millions of Americans. Afterward, the federal government established the Federal Deposit Insurance Corporation (FDIC) to insure bank deposits.

FROM "SOUND MONEY."

THE SITUATION; THE RESULT OF INTEREST-BEARING BONDS AND SHERMAN.

4.18: "The Situation: The Result of Interest Bearing Bonds and Sherman"
Source: *Sound Money* (Massillon, OH), August 22, 1895.

Populists looked to three pieces of legislation that rigged the monetary system against debtors. First was the establishment of the National Banking System in 1863, which put banking and currency policy in the hands of private (mostly New York) bankers. Second was the removal of silver dollars from the list of coins to be minted in 1873, which was quickly labeled the Crime of '73. Without this action, the large silver deposits discovered later that year would have reversed deflation. Thirdly, Populists also blamed the repeal of the Sherman Silver Purchase Act in 1893 for making the depression that started that year even worse. John Sherman, the author of the Purchase Act, supported its repeal. Each event contributed to the deflation of the late nineteenth century that impoverished debtors by making the money they owed harder to pay off. Notice that debt is not the laborer's only burden; the ball and chain attached to his leg is labeled "Interest."

THE MODERN HERCULES.

It is Life or Death—the Struggle Cannot be Avoided.

4.19: "The Modern Hercules"
Source: *Rocky Mountain News* (Denver, CO), November 18, 1894.

In this illustration by Wilbur Steele, the People's Party is seen as a modern Hercules taking on the old parties, which are strangling commerce and labor. The heads of the snakes are a triumvirate of Republicans led by former president Benjamin Harrison and Democrat Grover Cleveland. The word "contraction" refers to reducing the amount of money in circulation with the repeal of the Sherman Silver Purchase Act of 1890. Until July 1896, both the Republican and Democratic Parties had endorsed the gold standard. This left the People's Party as the only major party committed to free silver as a means of reversing deflation.

THE FARMER AND DEMONETIZATION.

The above table illustrates the relation between the current price of silver and the market price of the staple products of the farm. The figures given are the average quotations for each year. They plainly show the cause of agricultural depression, and explain the burden of rural indebtedness, with interest exactions and mortgage foreclosures that are fast changing American farm property into tenant holdings. The table also explains the conditions that have blighted thousands of prosperous and happy homes and reduced the inmates to wretchedness and want—a contrast that is depicted by the artist in the accompanying sketches.

4.20: "The Farmer and Demonetization"
Source: *Southern Mercury* (Dallas, TX), October 19, 1893.

Money proved to be the Populist Party's most important issue. Late nineteenth-century America suffered massive deflation, which particularly hurt farmers in the South and West. The chart in the middle of the illustration shows the declining commodity prices caused by deflationary monetary policy, specifically the demonetization of silver with the so-called Crime of '73. In the left and right panels, the artist contrasts a proud- and prosperous-looking farmer who was able to provide for his family in 1873 with the same farmer who loses his farm to a sheriff's sale (presumably for unpaid debts) in 1893. Populists called for both greenbacks (paper money not backed by precious metal) and "free silver" as anti-deflation measures.

THE GRANGERS' DREAM OF CHEAP MONEY.

THE GOLDBUG HIGHWAYMAN IS STILL AT WORK.

4.21 (left): "The Grangers' Dream of Cheap Money"
Source: *Puck (New York City),* July 8, 1891.

Opponents of Populism ridiculed its monetary proposals as giving farmers some-thing for nothing. In this cartoon, which ran in the New York City humor magazine, *Puck,* Grangers (members of a farmer organization that supported the Greenback and Greenback-Labor parties in the 1870s and 1880s) are shown hauling away bags of fiat money provided by Populist Senator William A. Peffer of Kansas. Anti-Populist car-toonists adopted Peffer, with his long flowing beard and archaic dress, as the symbol of Populism in order to portray the movement as hopelessly old fashioned. The ribbon flowing from Peffer's hat refers to the Farmers' Alliance. Although Kansas Populists had sent Peffer to Washington in 1891, the People's Party was not founded at the national level until 1892 (after the publication of this cartoon).

4.22 (above): "The Goldbug Highwayman Is Still at Work"
Source: *Rocky Mountain News* (Denver, CO), May 3, 1896.

Sometimes Populist artists made humorous revisions of opposition illustrations as a form of response to their characterizations. The original version of this cartoon by Joseph Keppler, which appeared in *Puck,* showed a slender, bearded bandit in western attire. Wilbur Steele of the *Rocky Mountain News* has replaced the bandit with the heavyset goldbug character. The goldbug highwayman's girth suggests he had grown fat living off the labor of his victims. According to Populists, the single gold standard hurt a wide variety of producers (represented as passengers from the coach) and impeded national prosperity (represented by the coach).

WILL WE SUCCEED?

4.23: "How to Lift the Burden from Labor"
Source: *Sound Money* (Massillon, OH), September 19, 1895.

In this cartoon, labor is trapped under the burden of mortgages, taxes, and low wages that vicious legislation has produced. The artist, Watson Heston, has placed Democrat Grover Cleveland and Republican John Sherman atop the burden in order to show both old parties are responsible. The Populist Party, represented as Jacob Coxey, is using the non–interest-bearing bond (greenbacks) as leverage to relieve the laborer while Shylock in the rear frets over the result. Coxey led a poor people's march on Washington, D.C., in 1894.

After President Cleveland secured repeal of the Sherman Silver Purchase Act in 1893, the United States floated a loan in Europe in order to recover some of the gold that had been paid out in international exchange. The bonds were in large denominations and sold only in Europe. Because the bonds were backed by nothing more than faith in the government's intention to redeem them, Populists argued that they were no better than greenbacks, which should have been circulated in the United States in small enough denominations for average Americans to use. If labor alone created wealth, money was only a method of keeping count and could be made of anything. All major industrialized nations today accept the idea that money need not be backed by precious metals, but the idea was controversial during the late nineteenth century.

THE UNICYCLE WON'T WORK.

Uncle Sam—I told you, **Grover, you** couldn't ride that darned one-wheel concern.   When you pick yourself up and brush off your clothes just jump on to this bicycle and you'll sail along like a daisy through the rest of your administration.

4.24: "The Unicycle Won't Work"
Source: *Rocky Mountain News* (Denver, CO), June 4, 1893.

Repeal of the Sherman Silver Purchase Act in 1893 made free silver the paramount issue of the mid-1890s. As the only political party committed to the bimetallic standard (gold and silver), Populists began to emphasize the issue unmercifully. It was highly popular in the South and West. In order to ridicule the idea of a monometallic standard (gold only), Populist cartoonists jumped at the chance to associate bimetallism with the bicycle and the gold standard with the highly impractical and difficult-to-ride unicycle. The 1890s has been called the golden age of bicycles; the first recognizably modern bicycle appeared in 1885.

SHYLOCK'S CURS AND THE PEOPLE'S WATCHDOG.

4.25: "Shylock's Curs and the People's Watchdog"
Source: *American Nonconformist* (Indianapolis, IN), September 17, 1891.

In this cartoon, Shylock is used as a metaphor for financial interests that controlled the Democratic and Republican parties. The People's Party, on the other hand, is the guardian of people's property (money, land, and produce), which Shylock desires. Notice the people's dog is blocking Shylock and his curs from reaching the halls of Congress where they could pass vicious legislation. Populists viewed special-interest legislation as the cause of most of the nation's problems.

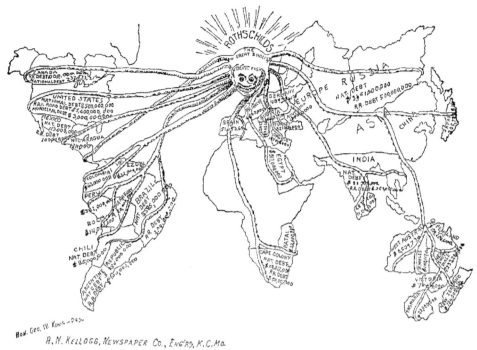

THE ENGLISH OCTOPUS—IT FEEDS ON NOTHING BUT GOLD.

4.26: "The English Octopus: It Feeds on Nothing but Gold"
Source: *Republic County Freeman* (Belleville, KS), June 16, 1892.

In this illustration, the English octopus is named Rothschild, the name of a famous Jewish banking family. Populist cartoonists employed both the English and Jews as symbols of hated financial interests. The nineteenth century was the age of imperialism. By the 1890s, it was said that the sun never set on the British Empire. This cartoon is used to demonstrate that colonialism had economic as well as political facets to it. Notice that the British octopus stretches to both the United States and Latin America, which were not part of the British Empire. The purpose of this cartoon was to show that both had become economic colonies of Britain, with all of the connotations for inequality implicit in European autocracy.

THE BLUE AND THE GRAY

"LET US CLASP HANDS ACROSS THIS BLOODY CHASM."--Horace Greeley anticipated the inevitable. The Farmers' Alliance takes up his burden twenty years after he laid it down.

4.27: "The Blue and the Gray"
Source: *Southern Mercury* (Dallas, TX), September 3, 1891.

Union and Confederate veterans shake hands across the bloody chasm created by the American Civil War, breaking the political loyalties that engendered single-party sectionalism. The sun rising in the background symbolizes the beginning of a new era of cooperation and reconcilement. As an electoral strategy, Populists attempted to form several coalitions. The southern and western sections of the nation had similar debtor economies. Both primarily produced low-value raw materials that were processed elsewhere. In turn, southerners and westerners purchased high-value finished products from outside the region. Inhabitants of both sections believed that railroads and northeastern financial interests unfairly exploited them. Civil War and Reconstruction animosities were the most important obstacle to cooperation because the West had been settled mostly by northerners. Still, this proved to be the Populist Party's most successful coalition.

GATHERING OF THE CLANS.--ON TO WASHINGTON. (VIA ST. LOUIS.)

We are coming brother toilers, we will trust in rogues no more;   All the thieves and thugs in office who have trampled on the right,
We have buried all dead issues and old grudges of the war;   Ho! Brothers, "up and at them!" let us once again be free --
We have bridged the "bloody chasm," and we'll bury out of sight   Cast out the plotting devils and drive them in the sea!
                                                                                                         --WATSON HESTON.

4.28: "Gathering of the Clans: On To Washington (via St. Louis.)"
Source: *American Nonconformist* (Indianapolis, IN), February 11, 1892; and *Southern Mercury* (Dallas, TX), March 3, 1892.

Populists hoped to overcome sectional animosities through the collective activities of producer organizations like the Northern and Southern Farmers' Alliances, Farmers' Mutual Benefit Association, and Knights of Labor. Here producers North and South are dropping their old grudges into the bloody chasm of Civil War animosities and are joining together under the banner of the People's Party to take hold of Congress. "Via St. Louis" is a reference to one of the early Populist organizing conferences that eventually led to the Omaha Convention in July 1892.

Money the Only Issue That Can Unite the North and South.

4.29: "Money the Only Issue That Can Unite the North and South"
Source: *Kingfisher Reformer* (Oklahoma Territory), May 17, 1894.

Westerners and southerners unite for political action in the People's Party in this illustration. The money issue held the best potential for uniting the West and the South. The nation had suffered from a quarter century of deflation by the 1890s. This meant that money was scarce and stayed primarily in the Northeast and Midwest, where the economy was more dynamic. Monetary policy brought the price of farm products from the West and South down below the cost of production by the mid-1890s.

UNITED WE STAND, DIVIDED WE FALL.
The Combined Forces of United Labor will Prove Invincible in their Onslaught

4.30: "United We Stand, Divided We Fall"
Source: *Southern Mercury* (Dallas, TX), December 24, 1891.

The second coalition Populists attempted to form was between farmers and laborers. Populists contended that they shared a common status as producers, which made them natural allies. "Labor vincit omnia" is Latin for "Labor conquers all." In this illustration, members of the Knights of Labor, Farmers' Alliance, and other similar organizations rally together. This coalition worked well in the South and West where both groups largely came from the same ethnic group.

Eugene V. Debs and Terence Powderly were the best-known labor leaders to affiliate with the People's Party, although Powderly eventually defected to the GOP. The People's Party appeared to gain ground in the more heavily ethnic Midwest and Northeast when John McBride, the Populist president of the United Mine Workers, defeated Samuel Gompers (who opposed Populism) for president of the American Federation of Labor in December 1894. Gompers, however, narrowly defeated McBride for reelection a year later. This was the only defeat that Gompers suffered between the founding of the AFL in 1886 and his death in 1924.

THE MODERN DAMON AND PYTHIAS

"United we stand: divided we keep right on paying the taxes,"

4.31: "The Modern Damon and Pythias"
Source: *American Nonconformist* (Winfield, KS), April 23, 1891.

In Greek mythology, Damon and Pythias symbolized the trust and loyalty of true friendship. The Knights of Labor and Southern Farmers' Alliance formed a warm and sympathetic relationship in the 1880s. Both organizations were prominent in the founding of the People's Party. Some historians have argued that this was an unlikely or doomed coalition because most farmers were property owners and most laborers were not. Populists argued that both were producers who were exploited by the same people and institutions. The Populist view of class pitted producers versus exploiters, instead of the Marxist concept of owners versus nonowners.

4.32: "I Simply Demand Justice! Where Is She?"
Source: *American Nonconformist* (Indianapolis, IN), May 5, 1892.

Populist farmers viewed laborers as coproducers, and saw their dilemmas as similar. In this illustration, mainstream institutions like the big-city press, colleges, the courts, and Wall Street proved unsympathetic to both. Populists contended that radicalism, like the anarchist movement, came from a sense of injustice that could not be relieved through normal channels. Worker proletarianization was a prominent symbol of the degeneration into European conditions that Populist farmers feared.

ADVICE TO STRIKERS.

The Best Way to Win a Strike is at the Ballot Box—Elect the Candidates of the People's Party Next November and There Will Be No More Cause for Strikes—Government Ownership of Railroads and All Other Public Conveniences is Coming and the Sooner You Make Up Your Mind to Vote the People's Party Ticket the Sooner Will Redress Be at Hand.

4.33: "Advice to Strikers"
Source: *Kansas Populist* (Cherryvale), August 24, 1894.

    In this illustration, the People's Party in the guise of Columbia offers the ballot box to strikers as the solution to their problems. Populists argued that popular control of government would benefit labor more than strikes, which disrupted the lives of innocent bystanders. The last two decades of the nineteenth century saw numerous labor disputes, many of which became violent. This scared respectable society and hurt labor's cause. Thus, the ballot box would provide labor with relief more effectively than strikes and/or violence.

He don't seem to enjoy it, but on election day
he votes for a continuance of the National Game.

4.34: "He Don't Seem to Enjoy It..."
Source: *Oklahoma Representative* (Guthrie), April 25, 1895.

In Populist farmers' appeal to laborers for support, third-party spokesmen argued that trusts and other monopolies hurt both elements. Propertyless laborers, however, had fewer resources to resist the encroachments of monopoly. In this illustration, the laborer is seen as a badminton birdie being batted back and forth by monopolistic interests who have grown fat at his expense. To stop the abuse, workers needed to stop voting for monopolistic interests.

HARRISON'S PROTECTIVE POLICY.

4.35: "Harrison's Protective Policy"
Source: *American Nonconformist* (Winfield, KS), August 2, 1888.

Populists shared the general West Coast animosity toward importation of Chinese laborers. They took labor's position that such immigrants depressed wages. The Pacific Coast economy was not as dynamic as that of the Northeast and Midwest in the 1890s. Republicans, in general, proved more favorable toward racial minorities, like African Americans and Chinese. Thus, Republican President Benjamin Harrison stands with Ah Sin in this illustration. Democrats, on the other hand, proved more favorable toward ethnic and religious minorities like the Irish, Poles, and Jews. Tippecanoe refers to Harrison's grandfather, William Henry Harrison, whose major claim to fame was victory over rebellious Indians at the Battle of Tippecanoe in 1811. Watson Heston drew this illustration for the *American Nonconformist,* which supported the proto-Populist Union Labor Party in 1888.

GROVER AND HIS SCARE-CROW THE PEOPLE FAIN WOULD GUY.

4.36: "Grover and His Scarecrow..."
Source: *American Nonconformist* (Indianapolis, IN), September 15, 1892.

The third coalition that Populists promoted was between African Americans and poor whites in the South. Both were economically depressed, but racism was the biggest obstacle to cooperation between the two groups. In this illustration, Populists make fun of a Democrat's attempt to use the race issue to unite white southerners.

Before World War I, 90 percent of African Americans lived in the slave states of 1860. Populist Congressman Thomas E. Watson of Georgia argued that "the accident of color can make no difference in the interests of farmers...you are kept apart that you may be separately fleeced of your earnings." It was difficult for white southerners to leave the white man's party less than two decades after the end of Reconstruction, especially when Republicans attempted to reinstate federal control of elections with the Lodge Force Bill of 1890. In the eyes of most white southerners, this bill meant restoration of Reconstruction. Blacks had similar trouble abandoning the GOP. Republican Party loyalties, racism, election fraud, intimidation, and even murder prevented Populists from receiving the majority of black votes. Despite direct appeals for interracial cooperation by Populist leaders that held the potential for offending the third party's rank and file, many white southerners still joined the People's Party. Democrats, however, defeated Watson for reelection in 1892 and 1894 through such outrageously fraudulent means that even prominent Democrats denounced them.

The Populist Trap and the Colored Vote.

4.37: "The Populist Trap and the Colored Vote"
Source: *Texas Sandwich* (Dallas), September 9, 1894.

   In this cartoon, which appeared in the anti-Populist *Texas Sandwich,* Democrats attempt to use the race issue to discredit Populists. The 1894 Populist state platform contained a plank calling for each race to control its own schools. Thomas L. Nugent was the third-party candidate for governor of Texas in 1892 and 1894. In this illustration, Nugent is flanked by two other prominent Texas Populists, James H. "Cyclone" Davis and H. S. P. "Stump" Ashby, while he attempts to lure the African American vote (black crows) with the school trustee offer. Norris Wright Cuney, the leading African American Republican in Texas, appears to be considering the Populist offer. In the end, Cuney remained a Republican, although Texas Populists made major inroads into the African American vote in 1894 and 1896. The covertness portrayed in this cartoon suggests illegitimacy.

McDonald—Say Gubner doan you hoal dat bait sech a distance in de future.
Culberson—That 's all right Bill.   All you have to do is to whoop up the colored vote for the democratic ticket and all will be well.

Illustration from *Texas Sifter*

4.38: "Charlie and Gooseneck Bill"
Source: *Southern Mercury* (Dallas, TX), October 22, 1896.

In the 1896 Texas elections, Populists were able to turn the tables on Democrats by contending William M. "Gooseneck Bill" McDonald, an African American Republican who bolted an 1896 coalition agreement with Populists, did so out of lust for a patronage appointment from Democratic candidate Charles A. Culberson. African Americans still voted in most southern states during the 1890s; thus, no party held any hope of victory without some black support. In their desperation to win the 1896 election, it was plausible that Democrats would have made such an offer to McDonald. African Americans generally saw patronage appointments as a means of recognizing their community in this era. Despite McDonald's portrayal as an ignorant rube, he was a fairly prominent banker and therefore had reasons other than patronage for opposing Populism. He did not receive the appointment, and may have never been promised the position.

WHAR DAT BILL COME AT?

4.39: "Whar Dat Bill Come At?"
Source: *American Nonconformist* (Indianapolis, IN), September 1, 1892.

Populists believed that appealing to African Americans on the basis of common economic interests was superior to the demagoguery of Democratic and Republican Party appeals. In this illustration, the African American voter is presented with a Republican admonishment to remain loyal to the GOP and a cynical Democratic statement that Democrats have always loved African Americans. The bill in question is the Lodge Force Bill of 1890, which would have placed southern elections under federal jurisdiction because of corrupt practices by Democrats. The bill never became law. A few western Republicans voted to defeat it in return for southern support on the Sherman Silver Purchase Act. Still, the attempt raised the specter of a return to Reconstruction that hindered the white exodus from the southern Democratic Party that Populists desired.

The Vampire That Hovers Over North Carolina.

4.40: "Negro Rule"
Source: *Raleigh News and Observer* (NC), July 4, 1900.

Reconstruction after the Civil War had been villainized throughout southern white society for more than a generation by the 1890s. This popular mythology contended that African Americans had dominated Reconstruction. Democrats argued that if whites divided, as they did with the Populist Revolt, then blacks would constitute the balance of power and reassert their dominance over southern society. The fear, of course, was irrational. Blacks had not dominated Reconstruction, but playing upon racial fears was one of Democrats' most effective means of countering Populism in the South. This cartoon from the vehemently anti-Populist *Raleigh News and Observer* portrays "Negro Rule" in the form of a bird of prey with an African American head as a threat to white families. North Carolina Populists and Republicans rode a coalition agreement to victory in 1894. Democrats won the state back with a reign of racial terror in 1898. This cartoon from 1900 shows the continued Democratic racial attack on fusion. Between 1890 and 1908, all eleven former Confederate states passed legislation disenfranchising African American voters.

4.41: "A Warning"
Source: *Raleigh News and Observer* (NC), August 30, 1898.

The Democratic Party–oriented *Raleigh News and Observer* overtly threatened the black community with violence in this August 1898 cartoon. While the "honest white man" holds only a ballot in his hand, the size of his clinched fist is designed to intimidate. Wilmington, the largest city in the state, had a black majority and a fusionist city government in 1898. Although fusionists lost the state elections in 1898, they maintained control of Wilmington's government. Shortly after the election, a mob of white supremacists rioted, killing numerous African Americans, and forced the resignation of the fusionist government. It is the only case of a successful municipal coup d'état in American history.

4.42: "Giving the Negro the Right of Suffrage..."
Source: *Ottawa Journal and Triumph* (KS), August 9, 1894.

Western Populists complained that the dominant party in their region manipulated the African American vote. In this illustration, prominent Republicans demean the black man while employing every possible method to secure his vote. "That shirt" (bottom right) refers to the "bloody shirt of rebellion," a reminder that Republicans fought the Civil War in order to free African Americans.

WESTERN REPUBLICAN WOLF—"Drop that nonsensical silver flirtation and be my bride. You will ruin the g. o. p. and yourself if you persist in your headstrong course. It's only a democratic scheme to bust up us republicans."

SOUTHERN DEMOCRATIC TIGER—"Hop into the ring with me, birdie, and quit your 'hollering' for silver. You will ruin the democratic party if you persist in your foolish course. It's only a republican scheme to bust up us democrats."

4.43: "Western Republican Wolf/Southern Democratic Tiger"
Source: *Republic County Freeman* (Belleville, KS), May 12, 1892.

Both the "Western Republican Wolf" and the "Southern Democratic Tiger" argue that the silver issue (and by association the People's Party) is designed to split the dominant party in each section, thus allowing the hated minority mainstream party to win. Arguments that a third party was an opposition ploy to divide one of the mainstream parties in an attempt to place the other mainstream party in power is a burden that all third parties have had to overcome. The American first-past-the-post electoral system strongly discourages party splits because the victor needs only a plurality, not a majority, of the votes to win. Arguing the People's Party was only a minority mainstream trick was designed to hold potential bolters to Populism loyal to their old parties. The success that Populists enjoyed under such circumstances suggests a significant degree of dissatisfaction with voters' former parties in the 1890s. By 1894, the People's Party was the largest or second largest political party throughout the West and South. The Democratic Party had collapsed in the West and the GOP did the same in the South. Because the argument made in this cartoon probably swayed some voters, Populist sentiment probably was greater than voting for the People's Party indicated.

Chapter 5

America's Destiny:
Apocalypse or Utopia

I N 1892, GROVER CLEVELAND AND THE DEMOCRATS captured the presidency
and both houses of Congress for the first time since the Civil War. Soon
afterward, disaster struck. The panic of 1893 and the depression that followed
were clearly the worst of the nineteenth century. At its nadir, economic activity
declined by about 25 percent. By the end of 1893, five hundred banks and sixteen thousand businesses had closed. Eventually, between 15 and 20 percent of
the workforce were unemployed and the prices for most farm products dropped
below the cost of production.[1]

The economy of Gilded Age America suffered from several flaws. Railroads
had overexpanded during the 1880s. Track laid where future traffic never mate-
rialized brought debt-ridden lines to their knees in the 1890s. Industries closely
linked to rail expansion, such as steel, consequently found their operations over-
extended as well. In addition, there was the ripple effect of a European depression
that had begun in 1890. The collapse of the London banking house of Baring
Brothers in that year brought a substantial call on collateral in the United States
that could not be met by 1893.

Northeastern fiscal conservatives attributed the panic to uncertainty about
the currency resulting from the Sherman Silver Purchase Act of 1890. Between
1890 and 1893, the redemption of treasury certificates caused federal gold
reserves to decline by nearly $132 million. Entrepreneurs came to question the
soundness of the currency and became timid in their investments, so President
Cleveland called a special session of Congress and, after an acrimonious debate,
secured repeal of the law in 1893.

Men of all parties in the South and West denounced Cleveland's repeal of
the Sherman Act. Since the Civil War, the nation's volume of business had tripled,

[1] Sperling, *Great Depressions*, 58–59.

while money in circulation had increased less than 50 percent. The resulting deflation caused economic hardship in the cash-poor outlying regions of the nation long before 1893. They argued that the American economy had run out of money, and that reducing the volume of money further would only aggravate an already desperate situation.

Repeal of the Sherman Silver Purchase Act provided Populists with a dramatic issue to promote. Because easterners dominated both mainstream parties, only the People's Party had endorsed free silver in its national platform in 1892. Populists thus labeled the repeal of the Sherman Act a Wall Street plot to make bankers rich. Federal expenditures, they claimed, would force deficit spending. Banks would purchase bonds with their reserves and place them with the U.S. Treasury as security for bank-issued paper money. The only difference between a government bond and a greenback, Populists argued, was the interest payments bankers secured. For Populists, however, labor, not slick deals, was the only valid source of wealth. Thus, government bond issues illegitimately concentrated money into the hands of the wealthy. In fact, the Cleveland administration issued the bonds in large denominations and floated them in Europe in the hope of reversing the drain in gold reserves. Certainly, the syndicate headed by banker J. P. Morgan that handled the European bond sales made a healthy profit.[2]

With the panic of 1893, millions came to know genuine privation. This appeared to create a greater empathy for the underdog and broader currency for the humane ideals of Populism. Establishment authorities, however, acted on the principle that Americans should support the government, not vice-versa. In December 1893, Populist governor Lorenzo D. Lewelling of Kansas requested that men "guilty of no crime but that of seeking employment" not be sent to the rock pile for vagrancy. This outraged Republicans, who quickly labeled Lewelling's plea "The Tramp Circular." Lewelling had already offended mainstream spokesmen by stating in his inaugural address that "survival of the fittest is the government of brutes and reptiles."[3]

In 1892, Ohio industrialist Jacob S. Coxey, a Populist, proposed that the federal government issue $500 million in non–interest-bearing government bonds (greenbacks) to state and local governments, upon the same terms that it loaned to national bankers, for the construction of roads. With no progress on his proposal by mid-1894, Coxey decided to "send a petition to Washington with boots on." Western farmers and silver miners proved to be his strongest supporters. The obvious sympathy inspired by the armies of Coxey supporters frightened respectable society. When Coxey attempted to deliver his petition to the

---

[2] Nugent, "Money, Politics, and Society," 125–26; and *Oklahoma Representative*, October 3, 1895.

[3] Lewelling's inaugural address and "The Tramp Circular" are reprinted in Pollack, *Populist Mind*, 51–54, 330–32.

president, police arrested him for walking on the White House lawn. Authorities expeditiously dispersed other "armies" as well.[4]

As the excitement over Coxey began to subside, new storm clouds appeared. George M. Pullman operated a railroad sleeping-car factory outside Chicago. In late 1893 and early 1894, he laid off 40 percent of his workforce and cut the wages of those remaining by 25 percent. In May 1894, Pullman's employees went on strike. When Pullman brought in strikebreakers, they turned to the American Railway Union for help. Union president Eugene V. Debs asked Pullman to submit the dispute to arbitration. When he declined, the class-conscious American Railway Union voted for a sympathy boycott, and union members sidetracked all Pullman cars. Railroad companies countered by proclaiming their contracts with Pullman prevented them from allowing their trains to move without Pullman cars. This stalled most rail traffic west of Chicago, including the U.S. Mail.

Attorney General Richard Olney, a former railroad attorney, quickly obtained an injunction against the strikers and President Cleveland ordered federal troops into Chicago to break the strike. The violence, which had been slight up to that point, then became spectacular. Mobs destroyed railroad cars, razed the roundhouse at the switching yard, and put part of the nearby Columbian Exposition to the torch. Although men not associated with the union did most of the damage, the strikers got the blame. The strike was quickly broken, the participants blacklisted, and Debs was packed away to prison.[5]

Coxey's movement and the Pullman strike provided Populists with a dramatic opportunity to assess what ailed the nation. Many believed they were witnessing the triumph of the liberty-killing autocracy that the Founding Fathers had warned about. As European autocracy crushed any sign of liberty, both at home and in their imperial pursuits, freedom appeared to be in jeopardy everywhere. Although Populists did not support anarchism, they believed the movement was the natural product of monarchy's unquenchable zest for absolute power. Third-party advocates openly sided with those resisting autocracy, be they American laborers or third-world victims of European imperialism.

Visions of catastrophe if contemporary trends persisted, and of utopia if citizens only took hold of their own destinies, did not remain uncharted territories of the mind during this period. Between 1888 and 1900, a flood of cataclysmic and utopian novels flooded the American market, representing a tidal wave of speculation about the future of the republic. The vast majority of the authors were Populists. Edward Bellamy's *Looking Backward* set off the flood; it told the story of America becoming a socialist utopia by the year 2000. Ignatius

---

[4] Coxey named his movement The Commonweal Army of Christ. For more on Coxey's Army, see Schwantes, *Coxey's Army*.

[5] For more on the Pullman strike, see Salvatore, *Eugene V. Debs*, 126–39; and Buder, *Pullman*, 147–210.

Donnelly's *Caesar's Column*, on the other hand, told of the downfall of civilization in a way that made the social critique he had written in the preamble to the Omaha Platform seem a desperate plea for civic regeneration.[6]

Populists hoped that the events of 1894 would bring a massive influx of urban laborers to their ranks. They firmly believed that a union of interests existed between farmers, Coxeyites, and laborers. Debs became a major third-party spokesman overnight. Embracing Populist rhetoric, he charged that the old parties "are controlled by the money power and both are equally debauched by its influence." Along with Jacob Coxey and Lyman Trumbull, one of the founders of the Republican Party, Debs came to symbolize the rapidly growing fortunes of the People's Party.[7]

In the congressional races of 1894, Populists increased their vote by 41 percent over their 1892 poll, despite the lower voter turnout of an off-year election. But the third party lost a large number of offices in the West where Democrats and Populists frequently failed to fuse. In the South, Democrats again won through fraud in Alabama and Georgia. A Populist-Republican fusion, however, carried North Carolina. In Washington, D.C., Republicans gained control of the House, while Populists held the balance of power in the Senate. With the election of 1894, the People's Party became one of the two largest parties throughout the South and West. This gave it major-party status in about one-half of the states of the Union.[8]

In the wake of the 1894 election, Democrats and Republicans in the South and West began a crusade to bring their national parties into line with popular sentiment in their regions. The American Bimetallic League, which silver mine owners had founded in 1889, generously financed their campaign. It sponsored several conferences in 1895 and 1896, as well as the publication of "Coin" Harvey's *Coin's Financial School*, which quickly became the *Uncle Tom's Cabin* of free silver. Reformers from all parties promoted it and many other tracts on the money issue during the mid-1890s.

Despite its increased ballot in 1894, the third party's loss of offices in the West appeared to make the chances for corrective legislation even more remote. In 1895, national chairman Herman Taubeneck announced that the People's Party would henceforth downplay the more radical planks in the Omaha platform and concentrate on the financial question. Party leaders subsequently promoted free silver as an entering wedge to gain control of government. The decision brought a chorus of howls from those committed to the entire Omaha platform. They feared that focusing on silver would divert the movement from issues that they

---

[6] Grant, "Populists and Utopia," 482. Also see Roemer, *Obsolete Necessity*.

[7] *Alva Review* (Oklahoma Territory), August 18, 1894.

[8] Tindall, "The People's Party," 17–21.

considered more important. The arguments of both sides, however, also revealed a pragmatic manifestation. Democrats in the South and West had been going over to silver in droves since 1894. Fusion with Democrats meant power in the West. Emphasizing an issue that the local elite embraced, however, would destroy the third party's rationale for existence in the South.[9]

[9] Ibid.

5.1: "The Gate to Honest Labor"
Source: *Anthony Weekly Bulletin* (KS), October 12, 1894.

Shortly after Grover Cleveland became president in 1893, America's worst depression to date began. Unemployment, labor conflict, and destitution ran rampant. Many believed that apocalypse was near. Populists laid most of the blame for the depression on the mainstream parties' fiscal policies. In this illustration, John Sherman, Shylock, and Grover Cleveland, whom Populists blamed for the distress, peer out from behind the gate. Sherman considered the Sherman Silver Purchase Act of 1890 to be a compromise that allowed the United States to avoid commitment to free silver. He became a leader in the act's repeal in 1893. The laborer and his family are faced with the choice of starvation and death or crime, prostitution, and ruin. Notice the artist's choice of having a buzzard named "Plutocracy" hovering over the closed gate.

MR. CLEVELAND TACKLES THE FINANCIAL QUESTION.

5.2: "Mr. Cleveland Tackles the Financial Question"
Source: *Anthony Weekly Bulletin* (KS), August 18, 1893.

This illustration humorously portrays the plight of President Grover Cleveland and Secretary of the Treasury John G. Carlisle as the banks in the background are destroyed. Cleveland is literally placed on the horns of a dilemma by the financial question, and it does not look as if Carlisle can be of much assistance. By the end of 1893, some five hundred banks and sixteen thousand business firms had closed. Many considered Cleveland's response to the crisis to be inadequate. Repealing the Sherman Silver Purchase Act did not restore investor confidence, but it did reduce the amount of per capita circulating currency, which made the depression even worse. Deflation continued until the end of the depression in 1897.

THE WHITE HOUSE CUCKOO CLOCK.

WASHINGTON, Oct. 18. Senator Morgan in his speech to-day denouncing presidential interference with the senate said: "But the trumpet has sounded, the forces were marshalled, the clock has struck at the White house, and the cuckoos have put their heads out of the box and responded, and informed us of the time of day, but they did not know what they were talking about, and did not take the pains to find out."—*Associated Press Dispatch.*

5.3: "The White House Cuckoo Clock" (above) and "The White House Cuckoo Clock—The Country Has 'Responded'" (right)
Source: *Rocky Mountain News* (Denver, CO), October 20, 1893.

These two cartoons ran side by side in the *Rocky Mountain News*. Northeastern financial interests convinced President Cleveland that a decline in investor confidence had caused the panic of 1893. The problem, they claimed, was an outflow of gold in foreign exchange payments caused by the Sherman Silver Purchase Act of 1890. Cleveland

THE WHITE HOUSE CUCKOO CLOCK.

The Country Has "**Responded**."

promptly forced repeal of the act. This made the free (untaxed) and unlimited coinage of silver at a ratio of 16 to 1 (the pre-1873 ratio) the most important political issue of the era. Repeal was highly unpopular in the South and West. In the late nineteenth century, Great Britain set the terms of international trade and demanded gold for U.S. Treasury notes. Repeal thus appeared to be primarily in the interest of British financiers. In these illustrations, Cleveland's supporters in repeal are viewed as cuckoo birds mindlessly chirping "repeal" to the beat of John Bull's hammer. Because free silver was one of the Populists' premier issues, they expected public opinion to turn against Cleveland and in their favor, as the right-hand illustration (above) indicates. Although many Democrats and Republicans in the South and West favored free silver, only the People's Party had endorsed the measure in its 1892 platform.

WHAT THE GOLD BUGS ARE DOING FOR UNCLE SAM.

5.4: "What the Gold Bugs Are Doing for Uncle Sam"
Source: *Kansas Populist* (Cherryvale), September 27, 1895.

This illustration shows Secretary of Treasury John Carlisle, Republican financial leader John Sherman, and President Grover Cleveland selling Uncle Sam to British financial interests. In January 1894, the Cleveland administration floated the first of several bond issues designed to bolster American gold reserves. Because Cleveland's purpose was to raise foreign gold, the bonds were issued in large denominations and sold secretly through the J. P. Morgan banking firm to foreign investors. Populists viewed this as favoritism to foreign speculators. Since 1790, U.S. bonds have been one of the safest investments in history, something speculators would favor during a depression.

Populists noted that bonds, like greenbacks, were backed only by faith in the credit of the federal government. If financial instruments that were not backed by metal were to be issued by the government, Populists claimed that they should be issued for the benefit of the common people. Specifically, they should be non–interest-bearing bonds (greenbacks) issued openly in small enough denominations for average citizens to use in their day-to-day business transactions. Notice that the artist, Watson Heston, has demonized John Sherman by giving him the horns and tail of the devil for seemingly reversing his position on the silver issue.

AFTER HIS SCALP.

5.5: "After His Scalp"
Source: *Puck* (New York City), August 19, 1891.

In this anti-Populist cartoon that appeared in *Puck*, "Sockless" Jerry Simpson and William A. Peffer are dressed as savages going after the scalp of John Sherman. Their knives are labeled "Alliance" because the illustration appeared before the founding of the national People's Party. By the mid-1890s, Sherman had been an impediment to inflationary monetary policies for years. His role in repealing the Sherman Silver Purchase Act would make him even less popular in Populist country. Notice that Simpson and Peffer have already taken the scalp of another Washington favorite, Senator John J. Ingalls of Kansas. Peffer replaced him in the Senate in 1891.

5.6: "American Representatives of the Rothschilds"
Source: *Kansas Populist* (Cherryvale), June 17, 1895.

American representatives of the Rothschild banking firm leer at the beautiful Columbia as President Cleveland puts her up for pawn. This is a reference to Cleveland's gold bond scheme to recover some of the yellow metal from European sources. Paying interest on the bonds, however, would have meant an ultimate export of wealth to Europe, especially Britain. The artist's portrayal of the bankers as unable to disguise their lust for the very desirable Columbia, the symbol of America, is a commentary upon Cleveland's allegedly treasonous pro-British policies.

A TALE OF TWO NATIONS.

John Bull Foolishly Endeavors to Sustain His Best Friend in America Against a Storm of Patriotic Sentiment.

5.7: "A Tale of Two Nations"
Source: *Anthony Weekly Bulletin* (KS), May 11, 1894.

In this cartoon, John Bull is seen working up a sweat trying to bolster President Cleveland's position in the face of criticism over the president's monetary policy, through the use of friendly northeastern newspapers. The arrows piercing Cleveland are free-silver arguments. The artist's purpose was to drive home the concept that the gold standard and its supporters were unpatriotic. While the label "Skatriotic American" appears to be an ethnic slur, it is interesting to note that the artist, A. V. Ullmark, was himself an immigrant.

THE damning treason can't be told of him who sells his land for gold,
And toiling millions yet unborn will hold this Judas' name in scorn!

THAT JUDAS FROM KENTUCKY.

5.8: "That Judas from Kentucky"
Source: *Sound Money* (Massillon, OH), April 3, 1896.

    Watson Heston shows Cleveland's secretary of the treasury, John Carlisle, as Judas selling Uncle Sam to the Jew, Shylock, for gold. Judas Iscariot, of course, betrayed Jesus for thirty pieces of silver, not gold. Yet Heston's use of Shylock and gold as a metaphor for the Jewish high priest Caiaphas and silver effectively labels Carlisle a traitor. The "Judas" epithet appeared regularly in the Populist literature of the 1890s in reference to Carlisle. He was a southerner from Kentucky where free silver was popular. Before the 1890s, Carlisle had favored the coinage of silver, although not free silver. Thus, his actions in supporting the gold standard as secretary of the treasury seemed treasonous. After his term in the cabinet ended, animosity toward him in his native Kentucky forced him to move to New York City, where he lived until his death in 1910.

THAT GREAT WAVE OF PROSPERITY!

Was to come around the bend just after the Holidays, according to Dun, Bradstreets and the township statesmen who got you to vote the old ticket "just once more," on their positive assurance that "Old Pros." was close at hand. While you are scratching for interest, taxes rent, saying nothing of a few new clothes for the family, if it won't give you the stomachache, suppose you read up, then *think a little* and next time John Sherman takes snuff, let him sneeze first—you "wait just once." If you *can't* think, don't try. This is a pointer for voters who can, that it is about time you were at it.

5.9: "That Great Wave of Prosperity!"
Source: *Anthony Weekly Bulletin* (KS), January 10, 1896.

Challenging the competency, and even motives, of those in power was a central facet of the Populist appeal. As the depression of the 1890s deepened, faith in the Cleveland administration declined everywhere. In this illustration, Uncle Sam is pleading for competent sailors to guide the ship of state, while John Carlisle attempts to summon help from John Bull, the symbol of Great Britain, with the lure of gold bonds. Notice the British flag waves above the American flag because those in charge are really working in the interest of the British. Labor has already jumped ship and the "Great Wave of Prosperity" that northeastern financial interests have promised with repeal of the Sherman Silver Purchase Act, in fact threatens to swamp the ship of state. The cartoon was meant to reinforce the ideas that the Cleveland administration was both incompetent and treasonously pro-British.

THE MONOPOLISTIC BEAST

5.10: "The Monopolistic Beast"
Source: *Sound Money* (Massillon, OH), September 26, 1895.

    Apocalyptic times seemed near by the mid-1890s, and Populists saw heartless capitalistic greed as the culprit. In this illustration by Watson Heston, greed is portrayed as a horrific monster devouring humanity. While Populists believed in a relatively free-market economy, they definitely would have put limits on greed in its most destructive forms. Their strongest following was among small, independent landowners. The People's Party also showed strength among laborers, small shop owners, and various other small producers. Antimonopoly was the glue that brought these various groups together. Business failures and farm foreclosures, plus the proliferation of monopolies, made the times seem apocalyptic for Populist elements by the mid-1890s.

WILL HE TOUCH IT OFF?

A Little More Injustice to Labor by Capital and a Bomb Will Explode Right
Here in These United States, Before Which All the Great and Holy
Revolutions of the Past Will Pale Into Insignificance

5.11: "Will He Touch It Off?"
Source: *Kansas Populist* (Cherryvale), June 1, 1894.

In this illustration, a capitalist is setting off a dynamite bomb with a torch labeled "Injustice to Labor." Bombs and dynamite were commonly associated with anarchists during the late nineteenth century. There was a general fear throughout the western world during the depression of the 1890s that capitalistic exploitation would eventually spawn anarchy and revolution.

HALT! SO FAR, BUT NO FARTHER!

5.12: "Halt! So Far, but No Farther!"
Source: *Rocky Mountain News* (Denver, CO), February 25, 1894.

   This illustration was inspired by Thomas Nast's 1878 cartoon entitled "Halt, Cossack," in which the centaur was a Russian closing in on a neoclassical building entitled "Civilization." In this rendition, free silver and the Populist Party are portrayed as the solution to the problems caused by the gold standard. In Greek mythology, centaurs were frequently seen as untamed, lower beings; thus, the artist Wilbur Steele villainizes supporters of gold as unnatural and inferior. In Colorado, where this cartoon appeared, free silver was not only a fiscal issue but also an important labor issue. Silver miners, whose livelihood depended to a great degree upon federal monetary policy, were the Populist Party's strongest supporters.

A LABOR DAY SOLILOQUY.

"What Does it All Mean?"

5.13: "A Labor Day Soliloquy"
Source: *Rocky Mountain News* (Denver, CO), September 5, 1892.

American industry witnessed more than 23,000 labor strikes between 1880 and 1900. Subsequent corporate and governmental suppression of labor raised serious questions about individual liberty and the future of the nation. In this cartoon, which is similar to a *Puck* cartoon blaming the depicted events on the McKinley Tariff of 1890, the workman ponders the meaning of the various labor disputes of the day that have ended in violence. Populists contended that popular control of government through the democratic process would secure laborers' rights better than direct action like strikes. Wilbur Steele obviously was a connoisseur of the works of other cartoonists.

CARNEGIE: *I simply press the button—Pinkerton does the rest.*

5.14: "Pinkerton's Thirty Thousand Thugs"
Source: *American Nonconformist* (Indianapolis, IN), July 21, 1892.

The Pinkerton Detective Agency provided private armies for corporate use during late nineteenth- and early twentieth-century labor disputes. In this cartoon, they are portrayed as brutes at the beck and call of industrialist Andrew Carnegie. This illustration appeared in the wake of the Homestead strike of 1892. In 1889, Carnegie had introduced his "gospel of wealth," an idea that justified great concentrations of wealth so the rich could contribute to philanthropic projects. Notice the relative sizes of the barrels labeled "Saved by Reducing Wages, 1882," and "For Charity, 1892." The illustration suggests the size of philanthropy was minuscule compared to profits, and the laborer preferred the justice he deserved instead of charity anyway.

WHO SAID COXEY'S WHEELS COULDN'T GET THERE?

5.15: "Who Said Coxey's Wheels Couldn't Get There?"
Source: *Sound Money* (Massillon, OH), October 31, 1895.

Numerous proposals surfaced on how to solve the problem of unemployment and end the depression of the 1890s. Industrialist Jacob S. Coxey of Ohio, a prominent Populist, proposed a scheme that would have the federal government hire unemployed workers to build roads. Others' proposals are treated as crashing off of Coxey's "Good Road" in this cartoon by Watson Heston, whose illustrations appeared fairly regularly in Coxey's newspaper, *Sound Money*. When no action was forthcoming from Washington, Coxey led a poor people's march on the nation's capital, "a petition with boots on," as he put it. But as Coxey attempted to present his petition, police arrested him for walking on the White House lawn and dispersed his "army." This outraged Populists, who pointed to his constitutional right to petition government. To Populists, Coxey's treatment symbolized the American political system's degeneration into autocracy.

THE OLD GAME.

But It Won't Work.

5.16: "The Old Game"
Source: *Rocky Mountain News* (Denver, CO), August 12, 1896.

Republicans like William McKinley, Andrew Carnegie, and Mark Hanna portrayed themselves as friends of the workingman, but the Homestead strike and low wages discredited them in Populist eyes. In this cartoon, the industrialists are drawn much smaller than the worker and his family in order to diminish their relative importance. Even though this workingman is a wage laborer, he is a producer, which Populists contended was superior to exploiters like the industrialists. In this illustration, Wilbur Steele portrayed the laborer as strong in defending his family.

EQUALITY BEFORE THE LAW.

Federal Judges Instruct Grand Juries to Favor No Man on Account of His Position.

5.17: "Equality Before the Law"
Source: *Rocky Mountain News* (Denver, CO), July 15, 1894.

In the wake of Coxey's march on Washington, the American Railway Union (ARU), led by Eugene V. Debs, called a strike against George M. Pullman's sleeping-car company. Railroad interests had been caught unprepared in an earlier confrontation with the ARU. In the interim, the railroad companies founded the General Managers' Association to coordinate anti-union efforts. When railroad workers, acting in sympathy with the ARU strike, sidetracked Pullman cars from trains used to deliver the U.S. Mail, the railroad companies invoked their contracts with Pullman and refused to allow the trains to move without Pullman cars. The federal government broke the strike with an injunction obtained under the Sherman Antitrust Act, even though the Act was clearly designed to break up business combinations like the General Managers' Association. In this illustration, the law in the pose of Columbia confronts the General Managers' Association on the unfairness of labor's treatment.

A NOTE OF WARNING.

All the active forces of the American Industrial Railway Union (1,000,000 strong in '96), K. of L. as well as the Legion and Alliance are People's Party men. It won't do for old party brigands to try their luck at holding up the People's Party train.

5.18: "A Note of Warning"
Source: *Alliance Gazette* (Hutchinson, KS), June 5, 1894.

This morale booster from the National Reform Press Association appeared in 1894. Here the Farmers' Alliance, Industrial Legion, American Railway Union, and Knights of Labor are seen running over corporate interests and mainstream politicians. The Populist appeal for support from labor appeared to be making progress by the mid-1890s. Notice the caption reads "Constitutional Rights, 1776," not "1789." Progressive historians of the early twentieth century argued that the Constitution of 1789 was a conservative step back from the promise of the American Revolution. These historians adopted a great deal of the Populist critique of American history. The direct link came in the person of Vernon Louis Parrington, author of *Main Currents in American Thought* (3 vols., 1928–30), who had been a Populist during the 1890s.

5.19: "Two of a Kind"
Source: *Rocky Mountain News* (Denver, CO), February 24, 1896.

Stereotypes of Populists as parochial in their viewpoint have been overstated. This *New York Mercury* cartoon was reprinted in the *Rocky Mountain News*. This suggests Populists kept up with world events as much as other Americans, particularly those events that verified the Populist view of Old World powers as corrupt and exploitative. This fit into their view of the superiority of America's republican institutions. Oppression of popular movements seemed to accelerate worldwide during the 1890s. The Spanish government sent General Valeriano Weyler to put down a Cuban independence movement beginning in 1895, and the first round of genocidal massacres of Armenians living under Ottoman rule began in 1894.

THE ANARCHIST IN PARIS.

He Must Never Be Permitted a Foothold in Free
America.

THE CHAMPION HYPOCRITE OF THE WORLD.

Let 'im bleed 'er Sam She's 'is."

5.20 (left): "The Anarchist in Paris"
Source: *Rocky Mountain News* (Denver, CO), December 11, 1893.

According to Populists, capitalist oppression inevitably spawned anarchism. One of anarchists' most infamous acts was to throw a bomb into the French Chamber of Deputies in 1892. This was particularly shocking to Populists because France was the only republic in Europe at the time. They expected anarchist assassination plots against autocratic governments, but attacking republican institutions suggested anarchists were getting totally out of hand. The sign reading "L.F.E" on the right stands for Liberté, Égalité, Fraternité (Liberty, Equality, Fraternity), the motto of the French Republic. In 1901, an American anarchist, Leon Czolgosz, would assassinate President William McKinley. Capitalist oppression spawning anarchist attacks seemed universal.

5.21 (above): "The Champion Hypocrite of the World"
Source: *Rocky Mountain News* (Denver, CO), March 1, 1896.

Britain, which in Populist eyes was the quintessential monarchy, is here seen supporting fellow monarchies of dubious character in their quest for domination. Britain had long contended that its imperialism was beneficial for subject peoples, both economically and by introducing Christianity to heathens. The size of the Turk and Weyler, representing Spain, in this cartoon suggests they are petty, although still vicious, powers. Cuba, a Spanish colony at the time, still needed Uncle Sam's protection. Freedom-loving people everywhere seemed under imperial attack.

THE BALLOT IS MIGHTIER THAN THE BULLET.

All laws made by representative, democratic governments, are but the crystalization of the ideas, wishes and demands of a majority of the people. Labor is largely in the majority in the United States and if united, could vote itself into power and make its demands the law of the land. Capital's hope of continued aggrandizement is based upon the expectation of the continued partisan division of labor's vote. Laborers must exhaust the remedy of the ballot, before appealing to the Winchester. -George C. Ward.

5.22: "The Ballot Is Mightier Than the Bullet"
Source: *Republic County Freeman* (Belleville, KS), August 11, 1892.

To Populists it seemed that innocents were being oppressed worldwide during the apocalyptic times of the 1890s. They held Europe as a counterimage to American freedom, justice, and opportunity. Rather than give in to violent reaction, the worker in a republic can use his ballot to stop corporate and governmental oppression. Populists expressed supreme confidence in the common people's ability to control government in a republic if they would only assert their rights.

READY!

Africa's Death Struggle.

5.23: "Ready! Africa's Death Struggle"
Source: *Rocky Mountain News* (Denver, CO), March 31, 1896.

Populists were particularly conscious of America's anticolonial origins and provided moral support to all subject peoples fighting European imperialism. England and Italy were seen as very threatening to those few African populations that were still independent. The title to the illustration suggests their cause is hopeless. The cartoonist's point was that liberty was under attack everywhere.

5.24: "The Great 'Christianizing' Nation Still At It"
Source: *Rocky Mountain News* (Denver, CO), March 23, 1896.

John Bull ignores the evangelizing mission of imperialism and simply takes up the collection in this illustration. The hat he passes among the third-world congregation is the pith helmet favored by European armies in the tropics, and it is held at the end of a rifle to show he is really stealing from the natives. Britain's hypocrisy is punctuated by the Christian messages written on the wall.

NOW IT'S ITALY.

What's the Matter With Europe, Anyway?

5.25: "Now It's Italy"
Source: *Rocky Mountain News* (Denver, CO), March 4, 1896.

Populists reveled in the difficulties European powers faced in their quest for empire during the 1890s, which suggested to them that other peoples were also willing to take up arms in defense of their liberties. In this illustration, Cuba has Spain treed, Abyssinia has Italy on the run, and the Boers (Dutch South African farmers) are repelling the English. Populist support for subject peoples regardless of their race was the product of Americans' commitment to self-rule and our long-standing opposition to monarchy.

CUBA, LIKE EGYPT, IS A VASSALAGE OF ROTHSCHILD

THE REAL REASON WHY CLEVELAND CANNOT RECOGNIZE CUBAN INDEPENDENCE

5.26: "Cuba, Like Egypt, Is a Vassalage of Rothschild"
Source: *Kansas Populist* (Cherryvale), April 17, 1896.

Rothschild, with Cleveland's blessing, appropriates Egypt and Cuba's wealth through bonding schemes that have the colonies' imperial rulers working for the Jewish banker. This cartoon blends anti-imperialism and monetary concerns. Populists laid blame for most of the world's problems at the foot of financial interests. The illustration was meant to explain why the Cleveland administration had turned a blind eye to the plight of neighboring Cubans: he was in league with financial interests that opposed such intervention. According to Populists, the oppression caused by financial interests was worldwide, not just limited to America.

Chapter 6

The Battle of the Standards

THE APOCALYPTIC TIMES POPULISTS CAME TO ENVISION by the mid-1890s made victory in the crucial election of 1896 an absolute necessity. The nation clearly was at a crossroads. If the mainstream parties continued their dominance, American liberties would be suppressed, farmers and laborers would be proletarianized, and the future of the republic itself would be placed in jeopardy. To many, the Homestead strike, Pullman strike, and Coxey's Army appeared to point the way to America's future.

Populists, however, also could look to some promising trends. Defections to the third-party effort were growing. Eugene V. Debs, leader of the Pullman strike, and Lyman Trumbull, co-author of the Thirteenth Amendment, were the most nationally prominent defectors. There were a number of lesser mainstream party deserters, too. In Texas, for instance, former attorney general Buck Walton and ex-lieutenant governor Barnett Gibbs flamboyantly joined the third-party ranks. Cleveland's repeal of the Sherman Silver Purchase Act had made free silver, a Populist demand, the paramount issue of the decade, which accounted for a substantial increase in third-party balloting in the congressional elections of 1894. In the meantime, western and southern Democrats and Republicans worked feverishly to get their parties committed to the white metal, which was incredibly popular in their regions.[1]

By early 1896, the People's Party could, with some justification, look forward to a union of reform forces under the Populist banner for the November elections. Two related issues, however, potentially divided the third party. Some Populist leaders wanted to promote free silver to the exclusion of other issues. It came to symbolize opposition to the northeastern financial interests that manipulated the nation's fiscal policy in their own interests. These leaders believed the party's more radical demands hindered recruitment. Others saw narrowing the issues to free silver as a betrayal of the party's commitment to completely revamping the

---

[1] Miller, *Oklahoma Populism,* 97; and Miller, "Building a Progressive Coalition in Texas," 283.

nation's financial system and nationalizing the railroads, telephones, and tele-graphs. Free silver was only one issue and not as important as some of the others.[2]

Proponents of emphasizing free silver presented the issue as an entering wedge to further reforms in internal party debates. It pulled disparate reform groups together, and victory would set the stage for further reforms. Those com-mitted to the full Omaha platform saw party leaders as selling out for the offices they might acquire through fusion with mainstream parties if they reduced the party's platform to something old party politicians could embrace.

The second, and intimately related, issue Populists had to deal with in 1896 was whether to nominate a separate national ticket ("keep in the middle of the road") or fuse with one of the mainstream parties.[3] This issue had dogged third parties for decades. Certainly if both Democrats and Republicans endorsed the gold standard, as was expected, a national third-party ticket was foreordained. State and local parties might fuse where possible, but Populists would lead reform forces. The possibilities for success seemed good. Party spokesmen noted that the infant Republican Party had won its second national race in 1860. Of course, the Whig and Know-Nothing Parties were only faded memories by 1860. Democrats in 1896 still had the sitting president, although he was rather unpopular by this date.

In January 1896, the Populist National Committee made a fateful deci-sion to set the date for their national convention after that of the Democrats and Republicans. They believed that neither old party would nominate a free-silver candidate. Republicans dominated the region from Maine to Iowa, with only New York, New Jersey, Connecticut, and Indiana as possible swing states.[4] The gold standard was most popular in this section of the nation. Democrats, on the other hand, had a two-thirds rule for nominations that made a compromise can-didate acceptable to President Cleveland seem most likely. Populists thus could expect to pick up a number of bolting mainstream party silverites in the wake of the mainstream party conventions. Republicans obliged by nominating Wil-liam McKinley of Ohio for president on a pro-gold platform. But the Democratic national convention proved to be a debacle for Populists. President Cleveland had offended so many elements of his party that reformers overcame the two-thirds rule and nominated William Jennings Bryan of Nebraska on a free-silver plat-form. Bryan was a dynamic speaker and close to Populists in his native Nebraska. Thus, the Populist Party, which had boldly agitated the issues and constructed the

---

[2] Goodwyn, *Populist Moment,* 228–29.

[3] Fusionists and middle-of-the-roaders constituted the most important factions within the People's Party. Fusion usually referred to forming a coalition with the Democratic Party, although southern Populists occasionally fused with Republicans. Fusionists mostly were westerners. Middle-of-the-roaders opposed fusion and came mostly from the South. The phrase, "keep in the middle of the road," was an admonition to not go off into a coalition with either Democrats or Republicans. It was a call for party purity, not moderation.

[4] Calhoun, *Minority Victory,* 13.

organization that had brought forth the greatest electoral participation by poor people in American history, suddenly lost its position as the leader of reform to a representative of one of the old parties.

Had Democrats truly embraced reform or was this a subterfuge to win offices? This debate would dominate Populist ranks for the rest of the election. Western Populists went to the 1896 Populist National Convention at St. Louis committed to giving Bryan and his Democratic running mate, Maine banker and capitalist Arthur M. Sewall, their party's nominations. Many had already agreed to fusion deals back home. In the West, the GOP was the hated party of the elite. Southern Populists, however, had been the victims of Democratic Party outrages for years and placed little trust in its commitment to reform; they called for a straight Populist ticket. At the party's convention in July, neither fusionists nor middle-of-the-roaders were in a mood to compromise. A small compromise group promoting a ticket headed by Bryan but replacing Sewall with a southern Populist for vice president emerged. Because voters cast their ballots for presidential electors, Democrats would have to deal with the Populist Party or run the risk of dividing the free-silver vote. Although by far the smallest faction, the compromisers got their way by switching their votes back and forth between fusionists and middle-of-the-roaders. Although the result looked like a reasonable compromise, only a small portion of the party was committed to the result. Behind-the-scenes manipulations by both sides seriously divided the People's Party. Although state party officials later worked out fusion deals for presidential electors where they mattered, the trust between western and southern Populists that was necessary to sustain a national party evaporated in the wake of the convention.[5] Both sides seemed willing to destroy the party in order to get their way. The Populists' western-southern coalition had fallen apart.

Bryan stumped the nation in the cause of free silver in 1896. Reformers of many schools rallied to his cause, but his campaign scared business interests, who poured millions into the McKinley campaign. On election day, McKinley, the Republican Party, and the gold standard triumphed. Bryan carried the South and West, but was unable to crack the Northeast or Midwest. Free silver had little appeal to industrial workers who feared inflation would increase the price of necessities. Bryan's candidacy, however, did save the Democratic Party from going the way of the Whigs. Had easterners controlled the Democratic Party and committed it to gold in 1896, massive defections of silverites would have given the People's Party a serious chance of eclipsing it as the major rival to the Republican Party nationally. Instead, a significantly weakened Democratic Party survived, but Bryan's nomination did mean that the northeastern wing of the party would no longer dominate the party of Jefferson for the foreseeable future.

---

[5] Tindall, "The People's Party," 1723–24.

6.1: "Got 'em on the Run"
Source: *Anthony Weekly Bulletin* (KS), November 2, 1894.

As free silver became the most important issue of the era, Populists expected to benefit from the 1893 repeal of the Sherman Silver Purchase Act of 1890. This cartoon, which appeared just before the 1894 congressional elections, shows the Democratic and Republican Parties taking cover from the political storm that is brewing. The cartoonist, Andrew Ullmark, has chosen the Cinderella story to make his point. The two ugly sisters running from the brewing storm (representing the political revolt of the 1890s) are labeled "Republican" and "Democracy" (i.e., Democratic Party). An unseen Cinderella represents the People's Party, which is about to reap the appropriate rewards for its virtuous behavior. Although many individual Democrats and Republicans favored silver, only the People's Party had endorsed the issue in its 1892 national platform. Populists, of course, hoped that their party, like Cinderella, would experience a meteoric rise in status. They also frequently drew analogies between the People's Party and the early Republican Party, which won its second national campaign in 1860.

By the National Reform Press Association.
RESULT ELECTION RETURNS.

6.2: "Result Election Returns"
Source: *Anthony Weekly Bulletin* (KS), November 23, 1894.

This cartoon appeared shortly after the 1894 election and again employs the Cinderella theme. Democrats and Republicans are swept away by the political storm, which represents Populist victories. Democratic Party losses were catastrophic in 1894, but the Republican Party actually gained control of the U.S. House of Representatives with that election. The small Populist contingent held the balance of power in the Senate. Southern and western Populists took different lessons from the 1894 election results. Many western officeholders lost their bid for reelection because they failed to fuse with Democrats, as they had in 1892. On the other hand, southern Populists learned that straight Populist tickets, or fusion with local Republicans (the minority mainstream party in the South), could win elections. Thus, the stage was set for intraparty conflict over electoral strategy in 1896.

IN WHICH BOX WILL THE VOTER OF '96 PUT HIS BALLOT?

6.3: "In which Box Will the Voter of '96 Put His Ballot?"
Source: Kingfisher Reformer (Oklahoma Territory), November 29, 1894.

In 1894, the Democratic Party collapsed in the West. Its candidate for governor of Kansas received only 8 percent of the vote. Likewise, Republicans collapsed in the South, receiving, for instance, only 13 percent of the vote in Texas. Many Populists believed that a major shifting of political allegiance was at hand for the all-important 1896 elections. For their part, southern and western Democrats and Republicans began a desperate campaign to turn their parties to free silver in the wake of the 1894 elections. This cartoon, distributed by the National Reform Press Association just after the 1894 election, sets the stage for the 1896 campaign by emphasizing the Populist view of the three contenders.

WHAT IT MEANS.

The Coalition of All Reform Movements Under the People's Party Banner Will Certainly Result in Driving the Old Parties From Power.

6.4: "What It Means"
Source: *Kansas Populist* (Cherryvale), February 9, 1894.

Populists looked to a union of all reform forces under the People's Party banner for the epic election of 1896. Thus, the People's Party ship in the foreground has a flag reading "Reform Press Flagship." Although this cartoon appeared in early 1894, Populists had even more reason to hope for a uniting of reform forces in the People's Party in 1896. In order to promote reform coalition, the party's executive committee set the date for the Populists' national nominating convention for late July, after those of the Republican and Democratic parties. Both mainstream parties were expected to adopt pro-gold standard positions. In addition, the Democratic Party had a two-thirds rule for nominations that seemed to guarantee President Cleveland's followers would be able to block the nomination of a pro-silver candidate for the Democratic nomination. After the mainstream parties nominated pro-gold candidates for president, Populists expected a flood of pro-silver refugees from the old parties to join the People's Party.

THE PEACEFUL REVOLUTION.

6.5: "The Peaceful Revolution"
Source: *Anthony Weekly Bulletin* (KS), October 26, 1894.

This illustration predicts a Populist victory at the ballot box that would sweep away corruption and oppression. It was designed to bolster Populist confidence in their ultimate victory over the forces of plutocracy. Notice that those following Columbia (portrayed as the People's Party) are all wearing laborers' caps and carry swords labeled "Ballot." The crooks being scattered by their march are in suits and are labeled "John Sherman," "Usurer," "Bossism," and "Grover." Both Democrats and Republicans carry British flags to emphasize their loyalty to autocracy, and Populism's commitment to republicanism.

SWINGING 'ROUND THE CIRCLE.

Uncle Sam: "Grover, you'r making me dizzy; why don't you use both oars and go straight ahead?"—National Bimetallist.

6.6: "Swinging 'round the Circle"
Source: *Kansas Populist* (Cherryvale), May 1, 1896.

As free silver became the paramount issue of the mid-1890s, Populists and other pro-silverite cartoonists found innumerable ways of playing on the single gold standard and bimetallic gold and silver theme. Here a somewhat impatient Uncle Sam urges President Grover Cleveland to use both the gold and silver oar in order to drive the ship, U.S. Finance, away from hard times toward prosperity. The implication is that the Cleveland administration was obtuse in supporting the gold standard. Uncle Sam, of course, always has the best interests of the nation at heart. The cartoonist, Luther Bradley, was a progressive Republican who drew for a variety of Chicago newspapers in the mid-1890s. The *National Bimetallist*, a free-silver paper based in Washington, D.C., distributed this cartoon to Populist and non-Populist pro-silver newspapers.

"KEEP IN THE MIDDLE OF THE ROAD!"

Side tracks are rough, and they're hard to walk,
    Keep in the middle of the road;
Though we haven't got time to stop and talk
    We keep in the middle of the road.
Turn your backs on the goldbug men,
And yell for silver now and then;
If you want to beat Grover, also Ben,
    Just stick to the middle of the road.

Don't answer the call of goldbug tools,
    But keep in the middle of the road;
Prove that the West wasn't settled by fools,
    And keep in the middle of the road.
They've woven their plots, and woven them ill,
We want a WEAVER who's got more skill,
And mostly we want a Silver Bill,
    So we'll stay in the middle of the road.

6.7: "Keep in the Middle of the Road"
Source: *Republic County Freeman* (Belleville, KS), July 13, 1892.

Whether to fuse with one of the major parties or remain in the middle of the road and not veer off into a ditch to fuse with Democrats or Republicans had always been a major dilemma for Populists. This cartoon from 1892 shows Populist presidential candidate James B. Weaver leading the Populist masses to a third-party victory. He is ignoring the pleadings of two-faced representatives of the old parties. Benjamin Harrison in the oversized hat represents the GOP and Grover Cleveland represents the Democratic Party on the right. Both are contradicting themselves by telling different groups of voters what they want to hear. The cartoon would have been just as significant for the 1896 campaign. Most western Populists were fusionists by 1896 and looked forward to combining with the Democratic Party, which had provided the margin of Populist victory in their region in 1892. Most southern Populists fell into the middle-of-the-road camp. The Democratic Party was the hated party of the elite in the South.

A DESPERATE FLIRTATION.

Dear Mr. Pop, Let us Fuse.

6.8: "A Desperate Flirtation"
Source: *The Representative* (Minneapolis and St. Paul, MN), July 25, 1894.

In this cartoon, a flirtatious, but decidedly unattractive and desperate, "Democracy" (Democratic Party) seeks a fusion partner in "Mr. Pop." The circumstances seem illicit. As the out-of-power major party, western Democrats would become obsessed with making an electoral deal with the Populists for the 1896 election. The illustration appeared in Ignatius Donnelly's newspaper, *The Representative*. Donnelly, who had drafted the preamble to the Omaha Platform, was a middle-of-the-roader committed to promoting the 1892 Populist platform in its entirety.

THE SITUATION WITH THE G. O. P.

6.9: "The Situation with the GOP"
Source: *Sound Money* (Massillon, OH), June 30, 1896.

This cartoon by Watson Heston shows the Republican Party being led by William McKinley in Napoleonic dress. He is flanked by John Bull and Shylock, representing the financial interests that drive the GOP. The gold plank in the Republican platform and the free-silver lion on the other side of the abyss are represented as impenetrable obstacles for Republicans who met in convention first in 1896. As predicted, they adopted a pro-gold plank to their platform and chose William McKinley of Ohio as their standard-bearer, which Populists hoped would prove to be their downfall. McKinley's Napoleonic garb represents the autocratic sympathies of plutocracy, monopoly, syndicates, and other traitors in Populist eyes.

SHALL IT BE STRIKE OR SPARE?

The Question Addressed to the Populists.

6.10: "Shall It Be Strike or Spare?"
Source: *Rocky Mountain News* (Denver, CO), July 23, 1896.

Democrats met shortly after Republicans in 1896. In a tumultuous convention in Chicago, pro-silver western and southern forces surprisingly pushed northeastern delegates aside and nominated ex-congressman William Jennings Bryan of Nebraska for president on a free-silver platform. Bryan was close to Populists on several issues. Democrats subsequently argued that only their nominee could defeat the Republicans and the gold standard. Fusionists within the Populist Party took up the mantle of securing the third party's endorsement, too. Thomas Patterson, editor of the *Rocky Mountain News*, was a strong fusionist. He had long kept a foot in both the Democratic and Populist Parties, although he had committed himself formally to the People's Party. In this illustration his cartoonist, Wilbur Steele, presents the Democrat Bryan as the best chance to defeat the money power. He has his sword, labeled "Truth," at the Money Power's belly. Notice Bryan's vigor and the Money Power's softness. The Populist convention had to decide whether to destroy the oppressor (by commissioning Bryan to strike) or let him off.

TO THE RESCUE.

ALL MUST PULL TOGETHER.

6.11: "To the Rescue"
Source: *Rocky Mountain News* (Denver, CO), July 14, 1896.

In this cartoon, William Jennings Bryan, the Democratic presidential nominee in 1896, needs the assistance of Populists and Silver Republicans to pull Uncle Sam out of the shoals of monometallic destruction. With Bryan already nominated on a free-silver ticket by the date of the Populist national convention, logic seemed to dictate that other silver forces should come to his support. Populists held their national convention after those of the Democratic and Republican parties in 1896. They hoped to pick up the support of those disenchanted with their old party's pro-gold stance. With Bryan's nomination on a free-silver platform, Populists were left with the Hobson's choice of supporting the Democratic nominee or splitting pro-silver forces.

6.12: "Crown of Thorns"
Source: *Sound Money* (Massillon, OH), August 20, 1896.

Carl Browne, Jacob Coxey's son-in-law, was an admirer of cartoonist Watson Heston. He modeled this illustration on Heston's work for the *Truth Seeker*, a New York City freethinker magazine. The artistry is very similar to Heston's, although Heston almost never let his Populist and freethinker artwork overlap. In the cartoon, Republican campaign manager Mark Hanna, who has McKinley in his pocket, places a crown of thorns on Labor (represented as Jesus) while Rothschild supports the whole event. It is an obvious reference to Bryan's "cross of gold" speech at the 1896 Democratic National Convention, which ended with the admonition that "you shall not press down upon the brow of labor this crown of thorns, you shall not crucify man upon a cross of gold." The popular notion at the time was that the speech won Bryan the nomination.

The only way to move that Boulder is to throw away those old fashioned weapons.
- National Bimetallist.

6.13: "Unanimity"
Source: *The Representative* (Minneapolis and St. Paul, MN), August 12, 1896.

In another Luther Bradley cartoon for the *National Bimetallist,* the forces of reform unite in order to defeat goldbugism. They have laid aside jealousy, vanity, bluff, and selfishness to unite. It is an obvious call for those Populists who still had reservations about the third party's support for Bryan to unite all reform forces. The cartoon appeared in middle-of-the-roader Ignatius Donnelly's *The Representative.* Many Populists who were middle-of-the-roaders both before and after late 1896 got swept up in the Bryan frenzy during the campaign. The Nebraskan was a charismatic speaker who electrified audiences in the West and South with his oratory. Realistically, Populists had little choice other than to support Bryan by the date this cartoon appeared.

Men on the Donkey--Say, Mister! Won't you please endorse us?
Pop--Not jest yet! You fellows have deceived us too often! We can't afford to trust you: especially that feller on thar behin'. I prefer to keep in the middle of the road --Adapted from the Cleveland Press.

6.14: "Chicago Nomination"
Source: *Southern Mercury* (Dallas, TX), August 6, 1896.

The biggest impediment to Democrats' obtaining Populist support in 1896 was their nomination of Arthur M. Sewall of Maine as Bryan's running mate. Sewall was both a banker and capitalist. This made him particularly obnoxious to Populists and gave mid-roaders a strong argument against endorsing the Democratic ticket. In this illustration, Bryan, with Sewall in tow, asks for Populist support. Charles Nelan of the Democratic Party–oriented *Cleveland Press* drew this illustration. He obviously understood the problem of bringing southern Populists into the Democratic Party. The Populist in this drawing is Cyclone Davis of Texas, the most traveled orator of the Populist Revolt. He had made an eloquent plea for the Populist National Convention not to send southern Populists back to the party that had abused them so viciously.

THE STAND TAKEN BY TEXAS REFORMERS.

That's a nice little trick to sit on, but I want something to stand on with both' feet "

6.15: "The Stand Taken by Texas Reformers"
Source: *Southern Mercury* (Dallas, TX), April 16, 1896.

The Populist convention was highly acrimonious, and it seemed inevitable that westerners would bolt if Bryan was not nominated and southerners would bolt if he was nominated. In the end, the People's Party nominated Bryan for president and Populist Thomas E. Watson for vice president. It looked like a compromise, but in fact was the product of behind-the-scenes manipulations and thus pleased almost no one.

The Texas delegation was the most prominent and vociferous middle-of-the-road group at the 1896 Populist National Convention. Verbally, they had emphasized supporting the entire 1892 Populist platform. This illustration has the Texas Populist standing tall on a platform labeled "Omaha Platform," which rests upon transportation, land, and finance supports.

"AFTER YOU, SIR!"
6.16: "Resignations Received Here"
Source: *Rocky Mountain News* (Denver, CO), July 29, 1896.

At one point during the 1896 presidential campaign, Arthur Sewall offered to withdraw from the Democratic ticket in favor of Watson. Numerous Populists had claimed that Democratic representatives at the People's Party national convention had promised to replace Sewall with Watson if Populists would nominate Bryan. Afterward, Democratic leaders declined. Watson forever claimed that he allowed his name to go on the ticket only to save the People's Party from destruction.

UNCLE SAM'S DILEMMA.

It's a Lot Worse Than Solomon's Celebrated Case.

6.17: "Uncle Sam's Dilemma"
Source: *Rocky Mountain News* (Denver, CO), July 28, 1896.

Americans do not vote for president, but for presidential electors. Nominating Bryan but saddling him with Thomas E. Watson as his running mate, created two Bryan tickets in every state where the Populists were active. Both parties struggled with what to do about this dilemma. In this cartoon, Uncle Sam is presented with the dilemma of Solomon, with the baby representing the vice presidential nomination. The People's and Democratic Parties vie for recognition as the mother. In the end, fusion deals were made in every state where they mattered.

THEY MAY HOPE TO WIN BY IT

But They Must Reckon With the Good Sense of the People.

6.18: "They May Hope to Win by It"
Source: *Rocky Mountain News* (Denver, CO), July 25, 1896.

This Wilbur Steele cartoon shows "Napoleon" McKinley and his campaign manager, Mark Hanna, driving a wedge labeled "Populist Vice-Presidential Nomination" between the West and South. Both are presented in the bloated pose typical of Populist representations of plutocrats. The moneybag hammers draw attention to Mark Hanna's tactic of assessing financial support from Northeastern business interests for the campaign. Bryan and the Populists scared such interests; thus, they filled McKinley's coffers. The illustration was a plea for unity in the face of a well-financed plutocratic campaign, but the animosities engendered by the vice presidential nomination split the Populist Party into highly antagonistic southern and western wings.

On election day, McKinley, the Republican party, and the gold standard carried the election.

Chapter 7

The Demise of the People's Party

THE PEOPLE'S PARTY SENT ITS LARGEST CONTINGENT—thirty-one men—to Congress in 1897. Their presence, however, did not disguise the fact that the once powerful third party was on life support as a major influence in American politics. Republicans would control the presidency and both houses of Congress for the foreseeable future. In Kansas, Populists finally took control of the state government and passed a number of reform measures. Two years later, Republicans regained power and repealed most of those reforms. In the South, Democrats probably stole the 1896 state elections in Texas. Although a GOP-Populist fusion carried North Carolina, Democrats regained control of the state through a reign of terror in 1898. As an organized political movement, Populism met its demise quickly after 1896. Tom Watson's 1896 eulogy that "the sentiment is still there, the votes are still there, but confidence is gone, and the party organization is almost gone" proved prophetic.

Modern scholars have offered a number of explanations for the Populist Party's rather abrupt demise. One factor had to be the party's split into acrimonious fusion and middle-of-the-road factions. Party leaders spent more effort on recriminations for the events of 1896 than they did on evangelizing prospective recruits. Of the three major electoral coalitions that Populists attempted to construct in the 1890s, the western-southern combination was the most important and the most successful. Both sections had colonial debtor economies that the Northeast exploited. This coalition died with the Populist nomination of Democrat William Jennings Bryan as the third party's standard-bearer in July 1896. In the West, fusion with Democrats was vital to the election of Populist officeholders. In the South, the Democratic Party was the hated vehicle of elite control from which Populists had rebelled. Venomous charges of party treason subsequently filled the pages of the Populist press.

Progressive historians of the early and mid-twentieth century offered an economic explanation for Populism's rise and fall. In their eyes, hard times explained the rise of a party of protest, and an overdose of prosperity as America pulled out of the depression in the late-1890s seemed to explain the party's decline. Massive gold strikes in the late 1890s resulted in the increased supply of currency that Populists had demanded, but without legislation. This may have influenced some to return to their old parties, especially those committed to nothing more than free silver. Fusion in the West masked the rate of decline in Populist followers, but the party met almost universal disaster in the elections of 1898. This was particularly true in the South. But the rise in the price of cotton that eventually would bring a modicum of prosperity back to Dixie did not take place in time to affect the 1898 election results.[1]

The nationalistic fervor generated by the Spanish-American War of 1898 constituted another factor in the demise of the People's Party. Atrocity stories from the yellow press (scandal journalism) meant voters from all parties could support the idea of evicting the Spanish from Cuba. For Populists, the fact that Spain was a monarchy provided extra incentive to support the war. But wartime patriotism also diverted public attention from what was wrong with America to what was right. Monopoly capitalism should have become an even greater issue for the People's Party with the emergence of what business historians call the great merger movement, which began in 1895 and continued until 1904, but criticism of the national direction seemed treasonous while the nation was at war with a foreign power.

The Populist position on the Spanish-American War and imperialism has long been misunderstood. It has often been assumed that those who favored war with Spain were uniformly imperialists intent on creating an American overseas empire. Certainly this element dominated, but most Populists were strongly pro-war and anti-imperialist. America had been conceived in anticolonialism, and most of Latin America had adopted republicanism earlier in the nineteenth century. It was Cuba's turn, and many Americans believed that autocratic Spanish misrule justified American intervention.

In addition to supporting war with Spain, Populists provided significant verbal support for anti-imperialism elsewhere, especially Boer farmers fighting Britain's imperialism in South Africa in the late 1890s. But as to American imperialism, the denial of self-rule to former subjects of the Spanish empire (and Hawaii, which was annexed during the war) was another matter. Populist newspapers made great sport of the Darwinistic pretensions of imperialists who wanted to "civilize" the savage. They thoroughly expected capitalistic greed to destroy these virtuous native societies. Imperialistic fervor likewise played a role

---

[1] Hicks, *Populist Revolt,* is the most thorough Progressive interpretation of Populist.

in Populism's demise. Ideas about the inequality between white Americans and subject colonial peoples discredited the egalitarian emphasis of the People's Party.

The race issue in the American South also may have provided some impetus for, or at least hastened, the Populist Party's demise. The cumulative effects of stolen elections, charges of racial treason, and terrorist attacks caused many Populists to despair of ever winning any elections in the South. As the third party collapsed, accepting the Democratic Party's racial attitudes became the price of returning to the party of the fathers. Where racial demagoguery did not provide the desired results, military action by Democrats eliminated local black/white political coalitions.

Populism was the last stand of freeholders and independent laborers before being proletarianized. Although the People's Party drew heavily from earlier American traditions in its analysis of what had gone wrong with America, a number of historians have emphasized the modernism of Populist solutions.[2] Populist issues, like antimonopoly and a democratized banking and currency system, dominated reform movements of the early twentieth century. Populists accepted economic development, but demanded that it be made humane.

As the People's Party died, many disillusioned supporters dropped out of politics. This is part of the reason voter turnout in presidential elections dropped 30 percent between 1896 and 1924. Die-hard Populists nominated national tickets in 1900, 1904, and 1908. But electoral support for the once-powerful third party was minuscule. Congress contained no Populists after 1903. Others continued the egalitarian struggle by joining Eugene V. Debs in the Socialist Party. Many, however, returned to the reform wings of their old parties. A number of Populist demands became law during the Progressive era, namely monopoly regulation, banking and currency reform, and the graduated income tax. There are even similarities between the Federal Warehouse Act of 1916 and the Alliance's subtreasury plan. Populists had also advocated direct democracy with reforms such as the initiative and referendum. Reduced voter participation, however, made a mockery of those reforms.[3]

In the 1890s, three major parties vied for the allegiance of the American electorate. It was by no means certain which would survive the decade, given America's traditional two-party political system. The Democratic Party found itself in jeopardy as the party in power during the depression of the 1890s. But in the end, the party of Jefferson saved itself with the nomination of William Jennings Bryan on a free-silver ticket. The reform legislation of America's Progressive

[2] The latest book-length work emphasizing Populist modernism is Postel, *Populist Vision*. It won both the Bancroft Prize and Frederick Jackson Turner Award in 2008. For a critique of this book, see Miller, "Populist Vision: A Roundtable Discussion." Sanders, *Roots of Reform*, emphasized the Populist origins of some of the most important reform legislation of the Progressive era.

[3] Saloutos, *Populism*, 2.

era can be seen as a response to what Populists had criticized about Gilded Age America. But Progressive era reforms were multifaceted and sometimes contra-dictory. Many then and now find Progressivism to be rather disappointing in its reform accomplishments. Populism was much more focused than Progressivism in its critique of Gilded Age America and in its vision of how to revitalize demo-cratic control of the nation's economic and political structure.

OUGHT-TO-MOBILE; BUT IT DOESN'T

-Courtesy of Minneapolis Journal.

7.1: "Ought-to-Be-Mobile, But It Doesn't"
Source: *The Representative* (Minneapolis and St. Paul, MN), September 6, 1900.

Many Populists were very disillusioned with Bryan and his free-silver campaign in the wake of his 1896 defeat. The People's Party had sacrificed its independence and the goodwill of those voters it had recruited to the third-party crusade to support a losing campaign. The loss was devastating to Populist confidence. This cartoon from the 1900 campaign (when Bryan ran a second time for president) expressed the disappointment many Populists had with his lack of success. Notice the broken front left wheel labeled "Free Silver." In 1900, Bryan seemed to waffle on whether to make anti-imperialism or antitrust his primary issue. In this cartoon, which appeared in middle-of-the-roader Ignatius Donnelly's paper, *The Representative,* Republican Charles Bartholomew (Bart) portrays free silver as a dead issue and Bryan as opportunistic on the trust and imperialism issues. Because of the damage Bryan and his free-silver crusade caused by dividing Populists in 1896, Donnelly and his readers enjoyed seeing the free-silver issue die.

THE POLITICAL PUZZLE.

The Populist: Blamed if I can make out which end is goin' to do the waggin'.
—By Courtesy Minneapolis Journal.

7.2: "The Political Puzzle"
Source: *The Representative* (Minneapolis and St. Paul, MN), May 24, 1900.

Division into warring fusionist and middle-of-the-road factions severely hurt the People's Party in the wake of the 1896 elections. Each side pointed to the other's faults in such a vicious manner that evangelizing new recruits was impossible. The lack of unity, plus what in hindsight was a poor decision to fuse with Democrats, caused the Populist rank and file to abandon the party in droves. Bart jocularly presents the Populist dilemma in this illustration with the divided "Pop Party" as a two-headed dog. Fusion and middle-of-the-road Populists held separate conventions in Cincinnati and Sioux Falls in 1900. Since the two heads of the dog are faced in different directions, the party clearly is going nowhere. The Populist farmer in this illustration is in a quandary about which faction to support. The Republican elephant in the background is amused by the situation.

PROSPERITY.

TWO INDUSTRIES THAT SHOW ABUNDANT SIGNS OF REVIVAL

7.3: "Prosperity"
Source: *Norman People's Voice* (Oklahoma Territory), July 22, 1898.

This cartoon, which appeared in 1898, after prosperity supposedly had returned to America, suggests the upturn of the economy was not as strong as advertised. Mortgage companies and pawnbrokers are businesses that would thrive in hard times, when desperation led many to take out second mortgages or pawn valuables just to survive. Prosperity may have played some role in the demise of Populism. The price of some western commodities did rise a bit, but the price of cotton in the South remained low until after the November 1898 elections, which saw Populist candidates in Dixie lose badly. It would take World War I to bring any measure of real prosperity to either the South or West.

DAVID AND GOLIATH.

7.4: "David and Goliath"

Source: *The Representative* (Minneapolis and St. Paul, MN), February 1, 1900.

In this cartoon by Republican Bart, the diminutive Oom Paul represents the Boer farmers resisting British encroachment in southern Africa. Boers repelled a large British invasion force at the Tugela River in December 1899. Bart has drawn John Bull as a large, but soft, figure whom the Boers have handled in David-and-Goliath fashion. Populists could particularly appreciate an illustration showing Boer farmers striking down John Bull. As inheritors of the American republican tradition, Populists supported self-rule for those resisting European colonialism.

7.5: "The Gentle Bondholder"
Source: *Rocky Mountain News* (Denver, CO), January 15, 1898.

Populists found occasion to skewer financial interests in the frenzy leading up to war with Spain in 1898. In this cartoon, the "Gentle Bondholder" is unconcerned about the fate of the Cuban people under Spanish rule, but has an apoplectic fit when he finds out Spanish bonds may not be honored. Populists usually attributed opposition motives primarily to greed.

DID YOU DO IT?

7.6: "Did You Do It?"
Source: *Rocky Mountain News* (Denver, CO), February 17, 1898.

Uncle Sam asks the Spaniard in hand, "Did you do it?" Cuba was one of the last colonial holdings in the western hemisphere, and Spain had been attempting to put down a revolutionary independence movement on the island since 1895. As hardship and atrocities grew, so did American pressure on the Spanish. As anticolonialists, Populists supported Cuban independence. When tensions came to a head in 1898, President McKinley sent America's newest and biggest battleship, the USS *Maine*, to Havana Harbor to evacuate American citizens. When the ship blew up and sank, Americans were outraged and demanded vengeance. The resulting patriotism of the Spanish-American War of 1898 also played a role in destroying Populism. Criticism of the nation's leaders or institutions, the most important tool of all reform movements, seemed treasonous during wartime. Thus, reformers, including most Populists, usually muted their criticism or were silenced. The war turned attention away from the concerns Populists had advocated; instead, war hysteria came to dominate public discourse.

SPUTTERING TO A CLOSE.

7.7: "Sputtering to a Close"
Source: *Rocky Mountain News* (Denver, CO), May 5, 1898.

Populists viewed the conflict in Cuba as a struggle between the forces of republicanism and monarchy. In their eyes, this justified war to liberate Cuba. In this illustration, the republican revolution of the Cuban people snuffs out the light of monarchy. Note that Populist antimonarchial sentiments, which they once had directed at robber barons, have now been redirected toward the alien Bourbon dynasty of Spain.

THEY CAN'T PHASE HER.

CRADLE OF LIBERTY

After Raising a Family of Seventy Millions Columbia Isn't Worried by a Little Thing Like This.
—New York Journal

7.8: "They Can't Phase Her"
Source: *Rocky Mountain News* (Denver, CO), November 28, 1898.

The United States gained an empire in 1898 when Puerto Rico, Hawaii, and the Philippine Islands became possessions, and Cuba became a protectorate. The United States assumed the role of tutor in the ways of statecraft for these "inferior" peoples. As proponents of the Founding Fathers' anticolonialism, most Populists opposed imperialism. The nationalistic pride involved in empire building, however, served to mute many reformers. The People's Party did very poorly in the 1898 congressional elections and virtually disappeared afterward. This cartoon originated in Democrat William Randolph Hearst's *New York Journal*.

NOT A MEMBER OF THE FAMILY.
The New Girl—But HOW about that book?
The Lady of the House—I did not write that book.

7.9: "Not a Member of the Family"
Source: *The Representative* (Minneapolis and St. Paul, MN), June 6, 1901.

Republican Bart destroys one of the popular justifications for imperialism: the idea that assimilation would be beneficial to native colonial peoples. In this illustration, the Supreme Court denies the new girl's rights as a member of the family (i.e., citizenship). Populists like Ignatius Donnelly, editor of *The Representative,* were outraged by the denial of colonial people's natural rights in the wake of a war allegedly fought for self-determination.

The Goddess of Democracy Welcomes Home All Honest White Men.

7.10: "They Are Returning"
Source: *Raleigh News and Observer* (NC), September 16, 1898.

The cumulative effects of the Democratic Party's race manipulation in the South eventually took their toll on the People's Party. Poor white southerners had long been considered the most racist element of southern society. Populist leaders in the southern states had either solicited African American support for the third party or pragmatically tried to gain their electoral support through fusion with the Republican Party, or both. Democrats responded with virulent racial demagoguery, intimidation, and even murder. Resisting such tactics, possibly a majority of whites in the Cotton Belt states had voted Populist anyway. With the collapse of the People's Party, however, they had nowhere to turn politically but back to the Democratic Party, and accepting the establishment's racial attitudes was the price of returning. This cartoon from the anti-Populist *Raleigh News and Observer* expresses the joy Democrats felt at the demise of the People's Party. Notice the artist implies that those who remain intransigent are dishonest. Racism had become the standard by which all southern whites were judged.

Chapter 8

The Role of Cartoons in the Populist Revolt

THE POPULIST REVOLT OF THE 1890s was a product of the Democratic and Republican Parties' inadequate response to the problems caused by industrial and commercial expansion during America's Gilded Age. Ritual battles over Civil War issues and the tariff failed to sufficiently answer the issues of deflation, monopoly, railroad exploitations, the widening gap between rich and poor, or the inordinate power financial and industrial interests gained over the American political system. Populists latched onto a third-party tradition already present during the late nineteenth century and built a grassroots movement capable of seriously challenging the dominance of both old parties. According to one of their critics, Populists had an "earnestness, bordering upon religious fanaticism" that sustained their efforts through the travails of ridicule, demagoguery, and even physical intimidation until their issues could no longer be ignored.[1]

Populist journalism was a major factor in making the People's Party by far the most important third-party effort of the late nineteenth century. It provided an alternative viewpoint to the mainstream argument that all was well with America during the Gilded Age. Recent technological developments, like boiler-plate syndications and the photoengraving that made reprinting cartoons quick and inexpensive, empowered a poor people's movement by making available the tools necessary to challenge a much better financed and entrenched elite for control of the nation's destiny. Despite a lack of journalistic experience, Populist editors were able to perform the party's educational function effectively through the use of ready-print syndications, which usually included cartoons that struck at the heart of those rapacious entrepreneurs and their political minions who, in the eyes of Populists, seemed intent upon destroying the American republican experiment.

[1] *Dallas Morning News*, June 25, 1892.

Third-party journalism provided an alternative to the mainstream's monopoly over the information fed to the American public. Providing interpretations that challenged conventional wisdom was a vital part of rallying citizens to the Populist cause. Third-party newspapers educated the public on contemporary conditions, pointed out the failings of major public figures in addressing the nation's problems, and provided an effective organizational tool for furthering third-party action. Populist cartoonists used exaggeration and stereotyping (as do all cartoonists) both to inform and to shock potential supporters out of their complacency and even their despondency. They are at least part of the reason the Populist Revolt brought forth the greatest electoral participation of poor people in American political history. Eighty percent of America's eligible voters cast a ballot in the 1896 elections. Voter turnout has not topped 60 percent in the presidential elections of the past forty years.[2]

In the end, the People's Party failed to sustain itself as a major player on the American political scene. The third party faded with an alacrity that startled both contemporaries and later scholars. But while it existed, the party was a major threat to the political hegemony of the mainstream parties and business elite's control of the direction of American society. The party's goal was to provide the American public with a continuing alternative to the mainstream parties, perhaps even replacing one of them. The Populist fate, however, was to force the Democratic Party to make a major change in its orientation, adopting at least part of the Populist program in order to survive.

After 1896, Populist journalism declined rapidly. About three hundred delegates attended the February 1897 convention of the National Reform Press Association. A second NRPA meeting five months later saw the number of delegates cut in half, and only fifty showed up at the 1898 convention.[3] Those third-party newspapers that did survive for a while were far less likely to carry boilerplate syndications with cartoons. Ready-print cost money, and the purpose of the cartoons was to lure recruits. Bryan's nomination for president put Populists on the defensive. To survive they had to retain what they could of their following, but party officials spent more time on fighting among themselves than recruiting new converts.

The reform papers that had sustained Populism in its heyday, and especially the cartoons that had informed and enlivened its pages, receded rapidly after 1896. Coxey's *Sound Money* ceased publication in 1897. The *Kansas Populist* followed in 1898, and the *Republic County Freeman* in 1899. Ignatius Donnelly's *The Representative* died with its editor in 1901. By that time, the *Anthony Weekly*

---

[2] "National Voter Turnout in Federal Elections: 1960–2008," http://www.infoplease.com/ipa/A0781453.html (accessed June 28, 2010).

[3] *Southern Mercury* (Dallas, TX), February 25, 1897; July 8, 1897; and May 25, 1898.

Bulletin had affiliated with the Democratic Party cause. Those Populist newspapers that survived the longest after 1896 were most likely to have been in publication before the Populist Revolt, and had built a following over the years prior to the Populist Revolt that they were able to sustain for a while longer. Cuthbert Vincent (Henry and Leo's older brother) bought the *American Nonconformist* in 1896 and edited it until 1905, when he sold it. The paper had been founded in 1879 and became an agricultural journal in 1902. The *Southern Mercury,* which had been founded in 1882, remained Populist until 1905, when it switched its allegiance to the National Farmers' Union, a resurrection of the Southern Farmers' Alliance; it ceased publication in 1907. The *Rocky Mountain News* retained its independent political status after the Populist Revolt (it had affiliated with the Democratic Party before 1892), and ceased publication more than a century later in 2009.[4]

Of the major Populist newspapers, only the *Rocky Mountain News* and Donnelly's *The Representative* ran cartoons regularly after 1897. The *News* found an adequate replacement for Wilbur Steele when he moved to the *Denver Post* in the late 1890s. Many of the cartoons to appear in the *The Representative* were borrowed from non-Populist sources like the Republican-affiliated *Minneapolis Journal* or were reprints from previous years. In the wake of the Populist Revolt, Andrew V. Ullmark and Roger Cunningham focused on their careers as artists. Watson Heston continued his photography business until his death in 1905.[5]

Although cartoons associated with the People's Party movement of the 1890s disappeared rapidly after 1896, harpooning plutocrats became something of a growth industry in the early twentieth century.[6] In the antiparty atmosphere of the Progressive Era, they largely lost their role as a mobilizing force for a specific political party, although some socialist newspapers regularly ran cartoons. The muckraking journalism of the early twentieth century was generally nonpartisan. Still, the old Populist spirit could be found in many of the cartoons of early twentieth-century America because the old issues of monopoly, political corruption, and the widening gap between rich and poor remained.

The profession of Populist cartooning died quickly in the wake of 1896—it was a party tool that simply succumbed to the fate of the People's Party. But cartooning had served its purpose well in rallying support for the Populist cause. As the reform press declined, its educational and mobilizing function disappeared,

---

[4] Kansas Historical Society, "Newspapers," http://www.kshs.org/library/news.htm (accessed June 24, 2010); *American Newspaper Annual* (1897): 645; (1898): 74, 649; (1901): 80, 289; Ford, "The Invincible Vincents," 17; *American Newspaper Annual* (1896), 189, 749; and *Rocky Mountain News,* February 27, 2009.

[5] Bonner, "History of Illustration Among America's Major Newspapers"; *Jasper County Democrat* (Carthage, MO), January 31, 1905; *Carthage Weekly Press* (MO), February 2, 1905; and *Truth Seeker* (New York City), March 4, 1905.

[6] Press, *Political Cartoon,* 264–72.

which helps to explain why voter turnout in American general elections declined rapidly after 1896. It was the poorest who were the most likely to withdraw from the American political universe.

People's Party political education, whether from editorials, news stories, or cartoons, had informed farmers and laborers about the causes of their problems during the 1890s. Populist cartoons, therefore, played a major role in educating, legitimizing, mobilizing, and empowering a grassroots movement of poor people that seriously challenged the right of the Gilded Age's business and political elite to rule America in the name of the people.

Works Cited

Newspapers

Alliance Gazette (Hutchinson, KS)
Alva Review (Oklahoma Territory)
American Nonconformist and Kansas Industrial Liberator (Winfield, KS)
American Nonconformist (Indianapolis, IN)
Anthony Weekly Bulletin (KS)
Appeal to Reason (Kansas City, MO)
Carthage Weekly Press (MO)
Dallas Morning News (TX)
Emporia Gazette (KS)
Jasper County Democrat (Carthage, MO)
Judge (New York City)
Kansas City Star (MO)
Kansas Populist (Cherryvale, KS)
Kingfisher Reformer (Oklahoma Territory)
Morgan's Buzz Saw (Hardy, AR)
Norman People's Voice (Oklahoma Territory)
Oklahoma Representative (Guthrie)
Ottawa Journal and Triumph (KS)
Payne County Populist (Stillwater, Oklahoma Territory)
Puck (New York City)
Raleigh News and Observer (NC)
The Representative (Minneapolis and St. Paul, MN)
Republic County Freeman (Belleville, KS)
Rockdale Messenger (TX)
Rocky Mountain News (Denver, CO)
Sound Money (Massillon, OH)
Southern Mercury (Dallas, TX)
Territorial Topic (Purcell, Chickasaw Nation)
Texas Sandwich (Dallas)
Truth Seeker (New York, NY)

Other Sources

American Newspaper Annual. Philadelphia: N.W. Ayer, 1888–1901.

Appel, John J. "Jews in American Caricature: 1820–1914." *American Jewish History* 71, no. 1 (September 1981): 103–33.

Barthelme, Marion K., ed. *Women in the Texas Populist Movement: Letters to the Southern Mercury.* College Station: Texas A & M University Press, 1997.

Bonner, John. "History of Illustration Among America's Major Newspapers." In *Illustrating America's Newspapers in the 19th Century,* edited by R. Michael Wilson. http://www.wildwesttales.com/stories/chronicle5.htm (accessed May 25, 2010).

Buder, Stanley. *Pullman: An Experiment in Industrial Order and Community Planning, 1880–1930.* New York: Oxford University Press, 1967.

Burnham, Walter Dean. "The Appearance and Disappearance of the American Voter." *Electoral Participation: A Comparative Analysis,* edited by Richard Rose, 35–73. Beverly Hills: Sage, 1980.

Calhoun, Charles W. *Minority Victory: Gilded Age Politics and the Front Porch Campaign of 1888.* Lawrence: University Press of Kansas, 2008.

Cherny, Robert W. *American Politics in the Gilded Age, 1868–1900.* Wheeling, IL: Harlan Davidson, 1997.

Clanton, O. Gene. *Kansas Populism: Ideas and Men.* Lawrence: University Press of Kansas, 1969.

———. *Populism: The Humane Preference.* Boston: Twayne Publishers, 1991.

Dobkowski, Michael N. *The Tarnished Dream: The Roots of American Anti-Semitism.* Westport, CT: Greenwood, 1979.

Fischer, Roger A. *Them Damned Pictures: Explorations in American Political Cartoon Art.* North Haven, CT: Archon, 1996.

Folkerts, Jean. "Functions of the Reform Press." *Journalism History* 12, no. 1 (Spring 1985): 23–24.

Ford, Merrilly Cummings, comp. "The Invincible Vincents." Unpublished paper, 1978. Copy in Kansas State Historical Society, Topeka.

Glanz, Rudolf. *The Jew in Early American Wit and Graphic Humor.* New York: Ktav Publishing, 1973.

Goldberg, Michael L. *An Army of Women: Gender and Politics in Gilded Age Kansas.* Baltimore, MA: Johns Hopkins University Press, 1997.

Goodwyn, Lawrence. *Democratic Promise: The Populist Moment in America.* New York: Oxford University Press, 1976.

———. *The Populist Moment: A Short History of the Agrarian Revolt in America.* Abridgement of *Democratic Promise: The Populist Moment in America.* New York: Oxford University Press, 1978.

Grant, H. Roger. "Populists and Utopia: A Neglected Connection." *Red River Valley Historical Review* 2 (Winter 1975): 482.

Handlin, Oscar. "American Views of the Jew at the Opening of the 20th Century." *Publications of the American Jewish Historical Society* 40 (June 1951): 323–44.

Harter, Eugene C. *Boilerplating America: The Hidden Newspaper.* Lanham, MD: University Press of America, 1991.

Hicks, John D. *The Populist Revolt: A History of the Farmers' Alliance and People's Party.* Minneapolis: University of Minnesota Press, 1931.

Hofstadter, Richard. *The Age of Reform.* New York: Alfred A. Knopf, 1955.

Kansas Historical Society. "Newspapers in Kansas." ©2010 Kansas Historical Society. June 24, 2010. http://www.kshs.org/library/news.htm.

Lebsock, Suzanne. "Women and American Politics, 1880–1920." In *Women, Politics, and Change,* edited by Louise A. Tilly and Patricia Gurin, 35–62. New York: Russell Sage Foundation, 1990.

Lutzky, Seymour. "The Reform Editors and Their Press." PhD diss., University of Iowa, 1951.

Martin, Roscoe C. *The People's Party in Texas.* Austin: University of Texas Press, 1933.

McCormick, Richard L. "Public Life in Industrial America, 1877–1917." In *The New American History,* edited by Eric Foner, 107–32. Philadelphia: Temple University Press, 1990.

———. "The Party Period and Public Policy: An Exploratory Hypothesis." In *The Party Period and Public Policy: American Politics from the Age of Jackson to the Progressive Era,* by Richard L. McCormick, 197–227. New York: Oxford University Press, 1986.

McMath, Robert C. *American Populism: A Social History, 1877–1898.* New York: Hill and Wang, 1993.

McPherson, James. *Battle Cry of Freedom: The Civil War Era.* New York: Oxford University Press, 1988.

Miller, Worth Robert. "Building a Progressive Coalition in Texas: The Populist-Reform Democrat Rapprochement, 1900–1907." *Journal of Southern History* 52 (May 1986): 176–77.

———. "The Lost World of Gilded Age Politics." *Journal of the Gilded Age and Progressive Era* 1, no. 1 (January 2002): 49–67.

———. *Oklahoma Populism: A History of the People's Party in the Oklahoma Territory.* Norman: University of Oklahoma Press, 1987.

———. "The Populist Vision: A Roundtable Discussion." *Kansas History* 32, no. 1 (Spring 2009): 18–45.

Mitchell, Theodore R. *Political Education in the Southern Farmers' Alliance, 1887–1900.* Madison: University of Wisconsin Press, 1987.

Morgan, W. Scott. *History of the Wheel and Alliance and the Impending Revolution.* Hardy, AR: The author, 1889.

"National Voter Turnout in Federal Elections: 1960–2008." Infoplease. ©2000–2007 Pearson Education, publishing as Infoplease. June 28, 2010. http://www.infoplease.com/ipa/A0781453.html.

Nugent, Walter T. K. "Money, Politics, and Society: The Currency Question." In *The Gilded Age,* edited by H. Wayne Morgan. 109–27. Syracuse, NY: Syracuse University Press, 1970.

Official Souvenir of the National Convention of the People's Party at St. Louis, Mo., July 22, 1896. Milwaukee, WI: Robert Schilling, 1896.

Ostler, Jeffrey. *Prairie Populism: The Fate of Agrarian Radicalism in Kansas, Nebraska, and Iowa, 1880–1892.* Lawrence: University Press of Kansas, 1993.

Pollack, Norman, ed. *The Populist Mind.* Indianapolis, IN: Bobbs-Merrill, 1967.

Postel, Charles. *The Populist Vision.* New York: Oxford University Press, 2007.

Press, Charles. *The Political Cartoon.* Rutherford, NJ: Fairleigh Dickinson University Press, 1981.

Roemer, Kenneth M. *The Obsolete Necessity: America in Utopian Writings, 1888–1900.* Kent, OH: Kent State University Press, 1976.

Saloutos, Theodore, ed. *Populism: Reaction or Reform?* New York: Holt, Rinehart, and Winston, 1968.

Salvatore, Nick. *Eugene V. Debs: Citizen and Socialist.* Urbana: University of Illinois Press, 1982.

Sanders, Elizabeth. *Roots of Reform: Farmers, Workers, and the American State, 1877–1917.* Chicago: University of Chicago Press, 1999.

Schwantes, Carlos A. *Coxey's Army: An American Odyssey.* Lincoln: University of Nebraska Press, 1985.

Shalhope, Robert E. *The Roots of Democracy: American Thought and Culture, 1760–1800.* Boston, MA: Twayne, 1990.

———. "Toward a Republican Synthesis: The Emergence of an Understanding of Republicanism in American Historiography." *William and Mary Quarterly* 29 (January 1972): 49–80.

Shannon, Fred A. *The Farmer's Last Frontier: Agriculture, 1860–1897.* New York: Holt, Rinehart, and Winston, 1945.

Shoemaker, Pamela J. "The Perceived Legitimacy of Deviant Political Groups: Two Experiments on Media Effects." *Communication Research* 9 (April 1982): 249–85.

Smith, Henry Nash. *Virgin Land: The American West as Symbol and Myth.* Cambridge, MA: Harvard University Press, 1950.

Sperling, John. *Great Depressions: 1837–1844, 1893–1897, 1929–1939.* Glenview, IL: Scott, Foreman, 1966.

Tindall, George B. "The People's Party." In *History of United States Political Parties,* by Arthur M. Schlesinger. 1699–1734. New York: Chelsea House, 1973.

Twain, Mark. *The Gilded Age: A Tale of Today.* Hartford: American Publishing Co., 1873.

U.S. Bureau of the Census. *Historical Statistics of the United States: Colonial Times to 1957.* Washington DC: Government Printing Office, 1960.

Ward, H. Snowden, and Catherine Weed Ward, eds. *Process Photogram,* vol. 5. London: Dawbarn & Ward, 1898.

Watson, Thomas E. "The Negro Question in the South." *Arena* 6 (October 1892): 540–50.

White, William Allen. *The Autobiography of William Allen White.* New York: Macmillan, 1946.

Woodward, C. Vann. *Origins of the New South, 1877–1913.* Baton Rouge: Louisiana State University Press, 1951.

———. "The Populist Heritage and the Intellectual." In *The Burden of Southern History,* by C. Vann Woodward, 141–66. New York: Vintage, 1960.

About the Author

Worth Robert Miller is professor of history at Missouri State University. He is a specialist on the Gilded Age and Progressive Era, and has written extensively on the Populist movement of the 1890s. His publications include *Oklahoma Populism: A History of the People's Party in the Oklahoma Territory* (University of Oklahoma Press, 1987); "A Centennial Historiography of American Populism," *Kansas History* 16, no. 1 (Spring 1993): 54–69; "The Lost World of Gilded Age Politics." *Journal of the Gilded Age and Progressive Era* 1, no. 1 (January 2002): 49–67; and "Building a Populist Coalition in Texas, 1892–1896," Journal of Southern History 74, no. 2 (May 2008): 255–96 (co-authored with Stacy G. Ulbig). Professor Miller also is editor of a Populism website that contains the most extensive bibliography on the Farmers' Alliance and Populist Party. It may be accessed at http://clio.missouristate.edu/wrmiller/Populism/Texts/populism.htm.

Index